VINEGAR

VINEGAR

A GUIDE TO THE MANY TYPES AND
THEIR USES AROUND THE HOME

JULIE TOWNSEND

CHARTWELL
BOOKS, INC.

This edition printed in 2007 by

CHARTWELL BOOKS, INC.
A Division of **BOOK SALES, INC.**
114 Northfield Avenue
Edison, New Jersey 08837

ISBN-13: 978-0-7858-2341-4
ISBN-10: 0-7858-2341-7

Printed in China

The benefits offered by the humble bottle of vinegar remain outstanding – in fact, no other liquid provides the human race with such an array of useful, practical, medicinal and appetizing qualities.

To investigate the world of vinegar fully can mean a wonderful adventure heading to the hills of Modena in Italy for research into balsamics, a segue to Orleans, France to sample wine vinegar, then crossing the seas with pickled cucumbers in a jar to fight scurvy as Christopher Columbus did, before reaching the shores of North America to follow the pilgrims tracking down apple cider vinegar. Once done there, you would set sail to the Pacific Islands to bask under palm trees, watching sap being drawn from the coconut palms to create coconut vinegar.

Your travels would involve a trip to Asia – to China for exotic oriental dishes, to Japan to eat as much sushi as you could, and to Korea to sample its kimchee, the vinegar pickle that accompanies every meal.

Heading to the UK, you could finally put your feet up and tuck into the old favourite of fish and chips with a helping of malt vinegar or non-brewed condiment.

While a world trip is not possible for most of us, this book offers you plenty of food for thought about vinegar, examining the many different types available, how each is made and where they can best be used, with recipes included. It traces the history of the condiment – as far as possible, since this universal ingredient seems to have existed always, with no known 'inventor' to quote.

It will provide you with a wealth of practical tips concerning its versatility as a cleaning, beauty, gardening and medicinal aid as well as many more uses. And if that is not enough, you can always put yourself 'in a pickle' by learning the principles and properties of vinegar as a preservative.

The only question that remains is what vinegar can not do. If it were not corrosive to metal, we would probably be fuelling our cars with it in an environmentally friendly mixture of energy-releasing bicarbonate of soda (baking soda) and vinegar. Meanwhile, there is plenty of scope for educational projects around the home, some of them using that exact same concoction.

So enjoy the many, many properties of vinegar in all its forms and uses, and keep that world trip in mind for another day.

Please remember that this book is for reference only. Consult your doctor about any medical condition first. The tips featured are home remedies only and every individual will have a different response to their complaint.

It is not known how vinegar was first discovered or who created it but it is documented in ancient texts from the Sumerians, Egyptians, Mesopotamians, Greeks and the Chinese – and was probably in existence before these eras. The oldest religious texts – in the Old and New Testaments, and the Koran – mention the liquid. The prophet Mohammed noted that vinegar is the best of condiments.

It is well known that exposing alcohol to the air will turn it into vinegar. It is also known that vinegar can be created from the juices of just about any fruit or grain – it can even be created with vegetables that are used to make alcohol.

So presumably vinegar wasn't so much invented by our ancestors as created by mistake.

It is also safe to say that in ancient times such a strong-tasting liquid would not have been discarded, instead a purpose would have been found for it. It is ironic that in days of old, without hospitals or the medical life-saving techniques now available, our ancestors were far more open to trying and tasting all manner of things as a survival strategy.

Today we are so much more cautious, believing that everything we eat

may, in some way, be trying to kill us. For the fact that vinegar has lasted to this day, we can thank our esteemed ancestors for their continued pursuit of discovery.

The disinfectant properties of vinegar would probably have been the most likely to have been observed prior to its culinary qualities. Vinegar was primarily used for its ability to purify and lengthen the lifetime of stored foods.

It is documented that pickled cucumber seeds arrived in the Tigris valley in Mesopotamia from north India in 2030 BCE. Babylon is reputed to have first used vinegar in 5000 BCE; the disinfectant and cleaning properties, as well as its ability to halt deterioration of food by acting as a preservative, are supposed to have been discovered by the ancient Babylonians.

The Sumerians, also in Mesopotamia, may not have understood the science of bacteriology as modern medicine does, but their knowledge has been passed down the generations.

Egypt was another prime user of vinegar, as a healing medication, disinfectant and preservative. There is a story that Cleopatra and Mark Anthony had a bet about who could consume the most expensive dish, so she dissolved pearls in vinegar then consumed them.

Cleopatra extolled the virtues of vinegar as a beauty treatment, and knowledge of vinegar's properties was used in the mummification process. Hippocrates, who lived in 400 BCE, was one of the first known respected physicians. He clearly understood the medicinal benefits to be found in vinegar and became a pioneer in the use of vinegar as medication. He found it could be used both internally as a drink and externally on the skin.

Creating a preparation of vinegar, lotus shavings, oil and water, he would apply this solution directly to wounds. He was also a great believer in a mixture of honey and vinegar for easing sore throats and alleviating respiratory ailments, and even used vinegar as an early form of antibiotic.

Physicians from the Middle East also employed vinegar. Between 721 and

1037 CE, the Arab physicians Jabir Ibn Haiyan and Avicenna (Ibn Sina) realized its disinfectant properties, its use as a clotting agent and ability to reduce inflammation and alleviate burns. They also advocated it for headaches.

Chinese medicine extols the virtues of vinegar for stopping bleeding

The properties of vinegar were also acknowledged in Chinese medicine. In the Sung dynasty, in China, vinegar was listed as one of the twelve items that no-one could do without and Chinese medicine extols the virtues of vinegar for stopping bleeding, increasing chi or qi (vital energy) and removing toxins. Vinegar is currently used for treating a variety of ailments. As recently as 2003, China used vinegar as part of the treatment for a pneumonia outbreak occurring across six cities.

The Romans drank vinegar for energy and refreshment – Caesar's armies consumed vinegar as part of their preparation for battle to keep them strong and fit. The beverage was known as posca, a mixture of water and vinegar made from grape or date juice, and was supposed to be a stimulant. Jesus is recorded as having been given a sponge soaked in vinegar by a centurion, which many believe was intended to torment him further, but perhaps provided relief.

In the Middle Ages, a wine vinegar industry sprang up in Orleans, France, where as many as 300 producers were operating. This eventually led to the creation of a guild, known as the Vinegar, Sauce and Mustard Makers of Orleans. The traditional method of balsamic vinegar making, which originated in Modena, Italy, gained popularity across Europe as people discovered the new and delicate aromas of this style.

Vinegar's disinfectant properties were put to good use during the various outbreaks of the Black Death (bubonic plague). People used it for protection against disease and thieves employed it to disinfect themselves when stealing from the dead. As sewage amassed in the streets in the 17th century, sponges soaked in vinegar were carried, which were held to the nose to block out the foul smell.

Ships at sea used vinegar to swab the decks and preserve foods – certainly Christopher Columbus's crew did so in 1492 on the voyage to discover America. Louis Pasteur's research into pasteurization and bacteria in 1864 led to extensive developments in vinegar production methods, opening the door to a new raft of industrial manufacturers.

In modern times, vinegar has been used to treat battle injuries. It has been hailed as an effective home remedy and has featured in countless recipe books. Now vinegar of all types is as commonplace as salt and pepper. It is amusing to think that the liquid Hannibal used to destroy boulders when sending his armies across the Alps is now a culinary ingredient that has stood the test of time.

The origin of vinegar itself is unknown. History offers no clue as to who first created white vinegar or how it was used but, for generations, women have passed down valuable cleaning tips using white vinegar and it was hailed as a domestic jack-of-all-trades long before proprietary cleaning fluids were available.

Typically found in most households whether at the back of the kitchen cupboard or under the sink, this vinegar is the most widely used in the home. It is also known as distilled, spirit or grain vinegar and is clear in colour with a taste that is considered harsh in comparison to other vinegars. Standard white vinegar purchased from supermarkets is quite acidic.

While it is used predominantly for cleaning purposes, it is still an important ingredient in some recipes.

Making White Vinegar

The white vinegar most of us use is likely to have been bought in a supermarket. It often consists of acetic acid diluted with water. The traditional process of making vinegar starts with a fermentation of rye or maize (corn) mash which is fermented with yeast to turn it into alcohol. The alcohol is then strained and distilled by heating it, causing the water content to evaporate as steam. The solution oxidizes and is then filtered, eventually creating a mild, diluted acetic concentration.

Commercial distilled vinegar is also made by filtering grape pulp through charcoal or even wood shavings. Large amounts of oxygen are then pumped into the alcohol mixture, which is then boiled to create a condensate, a vapour which is then allowed to turn back into liquid, when it finally becomes white vinegar.

This process is so fast that it can be completed in the space of a single day, which is why vinegar is so much cheaper to produce than many other types of distilled liquid.

How To Use

Home remedy – when the colourless liquid is added to water, white vinegar becomes a versatile cleaning product and disinfectant (see page 110).

Pickling – the sharp taste of white vinegar makes it useful for pickling and preserving. Strong foods such as onions and garlic combine well with white vinegar.

Recipes

White vinegar is no longer popular with modern chefs, who prefer milder and flavoured varieties, but it has featured in many cookery books over the years and its value is still strongly acknowledged. This is a traditional, tried and tested recipe for American Vinegar Pie.

Vinegar Pie with Vinegar Pastry
Makes 3 x 22.5-cm/ 9-inch pies

Vinegar dough
375g/10 oz/3 cups plain (all-purpose) flour
250g/8 oz/1 cup of butter
Pinch of salt
1 egg
5 tablespoons cold water
1 tablespoon white vinegar

Preheat the oven to 210°C (425°F). Rub the flour with the butter and salt until the mixture resembles fine breadcrumbs. Beat the egg and add the cold water and vinegar. With a wooden spoon, beat the liquid into the flour until the mixture becomes a smooth dough. Divide the dough into three; each piece should be enough for a 22.5-cm/9-inch pie. (Two pieces can be wrapped in clingfilm (plastic wrap) and kept in the freezer for up to three weeks.)

Roll the dough out into a 22.5-cm/9-inch circle about 1 cm/1/2 inch thick. Transfer the dough to a greased pie tin (pan) and trim the edges. Prick the bottom and sides of the dough with a fork.

Filling
3 eggs, lightly beaten
125g/4 oz/1/2 cup of butter
2 tablespoons white vinegar
50g/2 oz/1/2 cup plain (all-purpose) flour
1 tablespoon of vanilla essence (extract)
300g/9 oz/1 heaped cup granulated sugar
Pinch of salt

Preheat the oven to 170°C (325°F). Melt the butter in a saucepan then remove it from the heat and leave to cool slightly. In a food processor, beat the eggs lightly with the vinegar, sugar, flour and vanilla. Add the butter and blend until the mixture is smooth.

Pour mixture into the prepared pie dough and bake for one hour. The filling should be light brown when ready.

Beef Stir-Fry
Chilli Marinade

80 ml/ 2 1/2 fl oz/1/3 cup white vinegar
3 bird's eye chillies, seeded and chopped finely
1 tablespoon chopped (minced) coriander (cilantro)
2 garlic cloves, crushed
3 cardamon pods, crushed
1 teaspoon ground cumin
1 teaspoon ground turmeric
1/2 tablespoon chopped ginger root
2 teaspoons brown sugar
1 kg/2 1/4 lb lean minced (ground) beef
1 tablespoon oil
1/2 medium white onion, chopped (minced)

Combine all the ingredients, except the oil and onion, and leave to marinate overnight. Heat a wok to high temperature and add the oil. Add the chopped onion in a tablespoon of oil until soft. Add the meat with the marinade and stir-fry quickly to your taste preference. Serve with plain boiled rice.

If you enjoy cooking, Italian balsamic vinegar should be an essential ingredient in your larder. The question should be asked, however: is your bottle of balsamic traditionally made or commercially produced?

If it is tradizionale, cost and rarity will be the deciding factors as this vinegar is painstakingly made and slowly produced – in fact, the very finest balsamicos are held in the same high regard as vintage wines. This vinegar has a distinctive sharp and pleasant aroma and is dark brown in colour with a high acidity. The flavour is rich, sweet, sour and can be fascinatingly complex.

Balsamic vinegar originates from the province of Modena in northern Italy. The tradition of making balsamic vinegar has been handed down through the generations. It is one of the few vinegars that has been recorded in history – in 1046, King Henry III of England received a small cask of the vinegar from the Marquess Bonifacio. The folk of Modena continued its preparation, ageing it gracefully, sometimes over hundreds of years, in effect making 'vintage vinegar'.

The Estense family held a monopoly on the manufacture of balsamic vinegar from the 14th to the 19th century. They ensured that it was served at court banquets and grand occasions and the fame of this aged vinegar spread throughout Europe. Balsamic vinegar is now available across the world.

The only true and original balsamic is the traditional Aceto Balsamico Tradizionale di Modena which is subject to the strict controls of the Consortium of Producers of the Traditional Balsamic Vinegar of Modena.

Manufacturing Process

For many hundreds of years, wine was used as the basis for balsamic vinegar. In the late nineteenth century, new production techniques in Modena led to the ending of the traditional method and wine was replaced by concentrated must (grape juice) as the main ingredient. The grape has to be from the white Trebbiano vine stock, which is extremely sweet and sugary, and specifically grown in Modena.

The grapes are crushed into must as late as possible in the autumn, then slowly heated in open vats until the liquid comes to the boil. The juice is reduced by up to 50%-70%, creating an intensely sugary fruit syrup. The liquid is cooled, filtered, then poured into large barrels, allowing the sediment to settle.

It is decanted into clean wooden barrels and the 'mother of vinegar' is introduced (see page 66), assisting the slow fermentation. When the syrup is exposed to air, it turns into alcohol and finally into vinegar.

The next stage, known as the solera system, is what makes balsamic vinegar so special. The liquid is transferred into smaller barrels made from different types of wood and may be allowed to age for anywhere between three, five, twelve and – in rare cases – even 150 years. There are very strict rules on which types of wood the barrels for storing vinegar may be made of. Some makers will use only oak but variations of chestnut, mulberry, ash, juniper and cherry are also permitted.

Infusing the flavour from each of the distinctive woods is what makes balsamic vinegar unique, as the best is stored for years, gaining flavour from each particular wooden barrel. The complexity of the flavours creates a powerful and intense concentrate and, like a liqueur, it is an unwritten law that you should only ever use balsamic vinegar in droplets and not simply pour a stream from the bottle.

The maturing process for balsamic vinegar is exceedingly slow and, with the controls placed by the Consortium, the final yield is limited. Commercial producers have come to the rescue for the cheaper varieties, but they do not produce the same level of quality.

Commercial balsamic vinegars may start with concentrated grape juice or red wine vinegar, rather than the Trebbiano grape must, and additives such as caramel and sugar are used to enhance the sweetness. They are not governed by rules concerning the length of storage nor are they restricted as to the type of barrels used. In some cases, producers abandon wood altogether and store the vinegar in metal kegs.

These production methods nevertheless provide an economical alternative to traditional balsamic vinegar, supplies of which are limited. The cheaper varieties of balsamic vinegar are thus suitable for general cooking purposes. For anyone seeking the genuine Aceto Balsamico Tradizionale di

Modena, imitators are unfortunately prevalent, so to be sure you are getting what you pay for, look for the sealed, numbered bottle. This is from the Consortium of Producers of the Traditional Balsamic Vinegar of Modena, guaranteeing that the bottle came from Modena or Reggio and was made by craftsmen using the traditional methods.

There are two grades of authentic balsamic vinegar, one stored for a minimum of 12 years, the other for 25 years. While some vinegars may be even older, it is difficult to determine the age of a vinegar, hence the Consortium will only guarantee the product to be twelve or twenty-five years old. The validation process consists of several tests and ratings, working on a points system.

If the vinegar fails any of these, the sample is returned to the producer. If it qualifies, the balsam is bottled, sealed, recorded with its own history and given a number, all by the Consortium. As with vintage wines, research is the best method for finding genuine tradizionale balsamic vinegar.

How To Use

Tradizionale – use it sparingly not least because of its astronomical price tag; drops are best. Add it to the last stage of cooking to retain the fragrance and flavour.

For caramelizing – when cooked, the vinegar mellows further. It works exceptionally well for caramelizing vegetables or making marinades, stews and sauces.

With fruit – a few drops sprinkled over strawberries or other soft fruit produces a totally different flavour. Balsamic vinegar is delicious with tomatoes, either drizzled over sliced tomato salad or sprinkled into a tomato sauce.

With ice cream – for a sensational taste, sprinkle a few drops of the best balsamic over the finest vanilla ice cream.

Recipes

Balsamic vinegar combines well with many foods. It has a special place in northern Italian cooking, the recipes being passed down generations. Here are a few classic suggestions:

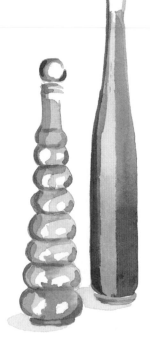

Balsamic Vinaigrette

125 ml/4 fl oz/1/2 cup balsamic vinegar
250 ml/8 fl oz/1 cup olive oil
1 garlic clove, crushed
Juice of 1/2 lemon
Salt and pepper to taste

Whisk together in a blender on low speed until the mixture thickens. Serve as a salad dressing.

Strawberries

500g/8 oz/2 cups strawberries
3 heaped (heaping) tablespoons caster (superfine) sugar
2 teaspoons balsamic vinegar
Greek yoghurt

Hull the strawberries and slice them into quarters. Put in a bowl and toss with the sugar until the strawberries are thoroughly coated.

A good wine makes a good vinegar

Leave for 20 minutes and then sprinkle with the balsamic vinegar and stir. Serve with a dollop of Greek or Greek-style yoghurt.

Tomato Salsa

6 small plum tomatoes
4 shallots
3 teaspoons balsamic
vinegar
3 teaspoons lime juice

Chop (mince) the tomatoes
and shallots finely, then
add the vinegar and lime
juice. Mix together in a
bowl.
Serve as a side dish or as
a dip with corn tortilla
chips.

Baked Lamb Chops

1 tablespoon olive oil
2 onions, sliced thinly
2 tablespoons balsamic
vinegar
2 tablespoons Worcester
sauce
1/2 teaspoon salt
1/2 teaspoon freshly
ground black pepper
1 teaspoon sweet paprika
1 teaspoon chilli powder
1 x 425g/15 oz can/ 2
cups chopped tomatoes
3 anchovies, chopped
8 lamb chops, trimmed of
excess fat

Preheat the oven to 190°C
(375°F). Sprinkle the oil in
a rectangular baking pan
and add the onions. Bake

in the oven for ten minutes.
Combine all other
ingredients except the
chops. Remove the pan from
the oven and lay the chops
evenly across the onions.

Pour the sauce over the
meat. Return to the oven
and bake for 1 1/2 hours.
Check every 30 minutes
and baste the meat with
the sauce. Then serve
with vegetables.

When Jack and Jill went up the hill and Jack came tumbling down, he went to bed and bound his head with cider vinegar and brown paper, it seems. From nursery rhymes to the present day, the healing properties of cider vinegar have earned it a reputation as the kingpin of home remedies.

There is evidence for this dating as far back as 400 BCE when Hippocrates advocated it as an antibiotic and healing elixir for patients. The Phoenicians valued its properties in the same way. Even during the Black Death, vinegar was widely acknowledged for its disinfectant qualities.

It was also used for drawing out poisons and preventing them spreading to other parts of the body. For poor Jack in the nursery rhyme, the cider vinegar would have drawn out the toxins from the bruising, reduced inflammation and disinfected the wound.

The benefits of apple cider vinegar have continued to be hailed in modern times, since it is claimed to assist in the treatment of many conditions, including weight loss, rheumatism and even as a cure for dandruff. It is reported to remove excess calcium from the body, making it particularly helpful in the relief of kidney stones and promoting blood circulation.

The key to apple cider vinegar is twofold: firstly, the naturally present mineral element potassium in apples promotes cell, tissue and organ growth; secondly, almost all of the minerals, vitamins and trace elements that the human body needs are found in the vinegar. Apple cider and cider vinegar are possibly nature's most perfect foods.

The liquid has a warm brown or dark caramel colour, a flavour like that of tart apples and a fruity taste which intensifies when cooked. This makes it suitable for adding to dessert sauces and for cooking other fruits.

The Balance Of Cider Vinegar

One tablespoon of cider vinegar contains:

0 calories
1g of carbohydrate
0 protein
0 cholesterol
0 fat
0 saturated fat

Making Cider and Apple Cider Vinegar

In the past, the preparation of cider vinegar and apple cider vinegar would have been similar. Today, however, the consumer is faced with choices from natural fermentation of fresh organic, crushed apples to commercial production using wood shavings, cores, peelings and other vinegars as the base.

The process of making your own apple cider vinegar is not complicated. A detailed recipe can be found on page 75.

Essentially, the juice of a large number of apples is boiled down until it reduces by half and then fermented to make a form of cider. To ferment, it should be allowed to stand in an open vessel for four to six weeks; the solution will turn into vinegar.

Apple Cider Vinegar Contains

Mineral and trace elements:
Potassium
Calcium
Magnesium
Phosphorous
Chlorine
Sodium
Sulphur
Copper
Iron
Silicon
Fluorine

Vitamins:
C
E
A
B1
B2
B6
Beta-carotene

Other variations in making cider vinegar involve a lengthy process of keeping chopped apples submerged in water for many months, adding yeast, then eventually allowing the mixture to ferment uncovered for four to six weeks, when it will become vinegar.

Some vinegars that are available commercially will have undergone similar processing but may not have used whole apples, and further distilling and filtering would have been performed to remove sediment and impurities. If an apple a day keeps the doctor away, a pesticide-free apple, offering almost all of the essential minerals required for healthy living – in addition to being fat- and cholesterol-free – is even better.

For this reason, it is sensible to consider seeking out organic apple cider vinegar if it is to be used as a home remedy. The label should state that the content is made from organically grown apples, that the process of creating the vinegar is traditional and that the producer has used the entire apple, not just cores and peelings.

Most organic farmers have adhered to rigorous procedures to ensure their product is pesticide-free, as required for certified organic produce. If you want to make your own apple cider vinegar, the recipe is simple but the process can take up to six months.

How To Use

There's more to cider vinegar than its medicinal properties – let's not forget cider vinegar's popularity in the kitchen.

Pickling – cider vinegar may colour the food in pickling, but the taste is milder than that of other vinegars and it produces delicately flavoured pickles.

Meats – ideal for fruity stews and adds flavour to fish and meat, particularly to roast pork and gravy.

Fruits – excellent for stewing fruits such as spiced pears and creating fruit sauces.

Drink – cider vinegar is famous for its cholesterol-lowering properties. The recipe for a cider vinegar drink can be found in the Home Remedies section of this book.

Recipes

Cider vinegar has become America's favourite vinegar, particularly as an addition to meat dishes, but the vinegar is popular in recipes from many countries.

Mixed Berry Syrup

750g/1 lb 10 oz/3 cups mixed blackberries and blueberries
750g/1 lb 10 oz/3 cups sugar
250 ml/8 fl oz/1 cup water
50 ml/2 fl oz/1/4 cup apple cider vinegar

Crush the berries in a pan and stir in the sugar and water. Simmer over a gentle heat for 20 minutes, stirring regularly. Remove from the heat and add the vinegar. Serve the sauce warm over pancakes or vanilla ice cream.

BBQ Sauce

75g/3 oz/1/3 cup soft brown sugar
3 garlic cloves, chopped finely (minced)
Salt and pepper to taste
2 teaspoons cayenne pepper
75g/3 oz/1/3 cup tomato paste
4 teaspoons Dijon mustard
350 ml/12 fl oz/1 1/2 cups cider vinegar

Place all ingredients in a saucepan and simmer until the sugar has dissolved. Keep stirring the mixture but do not let it boil. As soon as it is just below boiling point, remove from the heat and place saucepan in a chilled metal bowl to cool the liquid quickly. Use alongside grilled meats.

Pork Chops and Apple Cider

Pinch of mustard powder
4 pork loin chops, trimmed of excess fat
2 teaspoons olive oil
250 ml/8 fl oz/1 cup apple cider
125g/4 oz/1/2 cup soft brown sugar
125g/4 oz/1/2 cup cider vinegar
Salt and pepper to taste

Rub salt, pepper and the mustard powder into the chops. Heat the oil in a deep-sided frying pan until a cube of bread will brown in one minute. Add the chops and sauté them for five minutes on each side.

Mix the brown sugar and apple cider, add to the frying pan and reduce heat. Cook the pork chops in the simmering liquid for two minutes on each side, then remove the chops and reserve them.

Stir the vinegar into the juices in the frying pan and bring to boil. Continue stirring until the glaze reduces and thickens like gravy, about five minutes. Then turn off the heat and return the chops to the pan, turning them to coat each side in the glaze. Cover the pan and let sit for five minutes before serving.

While the Italians treat their balsamic vinegar like gold and the French take great pride in their wine vinegar, malt vinegar is by far the favourite in the United Kingdom – at the very least in the local fish and chip shop. Here you will find malt vinegar as the preferred condiment, sprinkled generously over chips.

Typically light brown in colour, malt vinegar's flavour is strong, with a hint of lemon. It has only medium acidity. The vinegar has culinary and medicinal uses. A cheaper substitute for malt vinegar is non-brewed condiment. This is 4%-8% acetic acid, manufactured using industrially produced acetic acid obtained through carbonylation of food-grade methanol and diluted with water. It may be coloured with caramel or left uncoloured, resembling white vinegar. This type of vinegar is clearly labelled as 'non-brewed condiment' as opposed to standard malt vinegar.

Non-brewed condiment was first used in England and Scotland in the mid-19th century, as a substitute for vinegar, with the rise of the Temperance Movement. The movement forbade its members to drink alcohol, even a few drops in a Christmas pudding, so it frowned on the use of vinegar since it was brewed from alcohol.

Making Malt Vinegar

The process of making malt vinegar is similar to the production process for making beer; a brewer can create a good malt vinegar simply by contaminating the beer liquid by exposing it to air.

Malt vinegar, like beer, is made from malted barley. The barley grains are first steeped in water to soften them and they begin to germinate, the natural enzymes activating the starch in the grain. The barley sprouts are then dried or heated to arrest their development and coarsely ground into a mash before being steeped in hot water to start the fermentation process.

The starch in the barley becomes maltose, a sugar, that dissolves into the liquid. Yeast is added and eventually the liquid, now known as gyle, begins a second fermentation. The gyle is stored in large vats, allowing air and bacteria present in wood shavings or twigs to finally convert the alcohol into acetic acid and become vinegar. Depending on the producer, the vinegar may be stored for many months allowing the aroma and flavour to develop and mature.

Turning the barley into the finest malt vinegar is a specialist practice so it is not surprising that most vinegar producers rely on 'maltsters' for their skills. Ensuring the barley is soaked for the right length of time, then dried, then soaked again, ceasing the germination process at the right time and heating to specific temperatures means that the creation of vinegar is an intricate process that can go horribly wrong.

How To Use

Pickling – very useful for chutney and dark-coloured pickles. Pickled walnuts were popular in Victorian times as was piccalilli. Both are coming back into fashion.

Toffee – see Kids Vinegar for a great recipe.

Sauces – great for meats, chicken and curries.

Home remedy – useful for curing hiccups and ridding oneself of onion breath.

Salad dressings – previously used for salad dressings, although the preference is now for balsamic and flavoured vinegar. Certain dressings still work best with malt vinegar.

Recipes

Orange and Mint Salad Dressing

2-3 teaspoons brown sugar
3 teaspoons hot water
50g/2 oz/1/2 cup fresh mint leaves
125 ml/4 fl oz/1/2 cup malt vinegar
4 oranges, seeded, pulp and juice reserved
2 tablespoons unsweetened pineapple juice

Dissolve sugar in water and allow to cool. Chop the mint leaves and combine with the vinegar, but take care not to turn it into a green sludge. Add the sugared water and pour into a bowl containing the orange juice and pulp and the pineapple juice. Stir to combine. Serve at once over green salad.

Old English Mint Sauce

1 tablespoon finely chopped mint
2 tablespoons malt vinegar
1 tablespoon brown sugar

Place all the ingredients in a saucepan and simmer for ten minutes, taking care not to let the liquid boil.

Add more sugar or water if required. Transfer to a sauceboat and serve, while still warm, with roast lamb. Stir before pouring.

Baked Chicken Drumsticks with Malt Vinegar

2 tablespoons vegetable oil
1 small onion, sliced
1 carrot, scraped and chopped
1 stick of celery, chopped
10 chicken drumsticks
2 tablespoons unsalted butter
75 ml/3 fl oz/1/3 cup malt vinegar
75 ml/3 fl oz/1/3 cup dry white wine
250 ml/8 fl oz/1 cup chicken stock
2 teaspoons dried thyme
2 bay leaves
1/2 teaspoon ground cumin
Salt and freshly ground black pepper

Heat the oven to 200°C (400°F). Use a baking dish with a lid. Grease the bottom of the dish with the oil, then add the onion, carrot and celery. Rub salt and pepper into the chicken legs for seasoning. Arrange the drumsticks in a layer across the onion and

Stir-fry Hot Chilli Prawns

Sambal oelek is an Indonesian spice obtainable from ethnic grocers and some supermarkets

2 tablespoons vegetable oil
500g/1 1/4 lb/2 cups uncooked prawns (shrimp), peeled
2 cloves garlic, finely chopped (minced)
1 teaspoon ginger root, finely chopped (minced)
3 teaspoons sambal oelek
2 bird's eye chillies, seeded and chopped
1 teaspoon Thai or Vietnamese fish sauce
2 teaspoons black bean sauce
1 tablespoon malt vinegar
2 teaspoons tomato paste
3 teaspoons brown sugar

chopped vegetables. Melt the butter and pour it over the chicken. Combine the vinegar, wine, chicken stock, thyme, bay leaves and cumin and pour the mixture over the chicken. Cover the dish and place it in the oven. Bake for 20 minutes, then turn the drumsticks over, baste them with the juices, continue to cook for another 20 minutes before basting again. Cook for a final 20 minutes. Serve with pasta or mashed potato.

Heat the oil in a wok until hot. Stir-fry the garlic, ginger, sambal oelek and bird's eye chillies with fish sauce and black bean sauce for two minutes. Add vinegar, tomato paste and sugar, stirring continuously for two minutes. Add the prawns, stirring to coat the prawns with the sauce, then cook until the prawn flesh is no longer transparent, about five minutes. Serve with boiled rice.

The origin of the word 'vinegar' is the French 'vin aigre' meaning 'sour wine' and indeed, if you leave a bottle of wine open to the air, it will eventually turn into vinegar.

It is not known who first discovered this process, but the standard method for making vinegar in France is much more sophisticated and is known as the Orleanais method. The process is very similar to that used by the makers of balsamic vinegar (though balsamic vinegar is not made from wine but from grape must). The French use the oldest vinegar-making process in the world, though Louis Pasteur's studies in bacteria and fermentation in 1864 somewhat altered it.

The production of wine vinegar began in Europe, specifically in France, Germany and Spain, although wine vinegars are now made throughout the world in any area that produces wine. The initial ingredient in wine vinegar is white wine and/or red wine, the more expensive varieties being made from champagne, sherry and pinot grigio.

Production of wine vinegar began in Europe, although it is now made all over the world

Wine makers have experimented further and now offer new styles such as Chardonnay, Cabernet Sauvignon and Muscat. In any case, wine vinegars are the chef's favourite condiment. White wine vinegar is pale gold in colour and red wine vinegar is a translucent red. Both have the aroma of wine and a sharp, acidic flavour, though white wine vinegar is milder and red wine vinegar more mellow. The colour of the vinegar can sometimes stain.

Making Wine Vinegar

Beginning with a good quality wine or blend of wines, the traditional or Orleanais method, explained later in this book, is to ferment the wine in partially full wooden barrels and allow it to acidify over many months into vinegar. The process is slow. Once the vinegar has formed, it is strained into other casks, allowing the flavour to mature with rich complexity. Wine vinegar may even be made from vintage wines, though this is not stored for the same length of time.

In 1864, Louis Pasteur's research into bacteria studied the process of vinegar's natural fermentation. While the traditional method allowed the wine to slowly turn sour over many months, Pasteur found that supplying more oxygen to the wine increased the speed at which it turned into vinegar. Commercial production uses Pasteur's principles, increasing aeration to enhance the rapid growth of bacteria.

A faster and more economical product was produced by 'trickling', the constant pouring of wine over wood chips to which acetic bacteria could cling, and in some cases using a poorer quality of wine. The Orleanais method offers a slower, matured vinegar with better flavour.

How To Use

Meats, vegetables and fruits – makes excellent sauces and dressing bases.
Flavoured vinegar – white wine vinegar is an excellent base for creating a flavoured vinegar. Combine it with any of the following: basil, bay leaves, chillies, fennel, tarragon and thyme.
Spiced fruit preserves – red wine vinegar is a wonderful accompaniment to preserves.

Recipes

Popularly the chef's choice, wine vinegar's tartness balances flavour, reduces the need for salt, helps avoid the use of cream and butter and has the advantage of being fat-free. It can be used with all the above, however, for some wonderful concoctions.

Hollandaise Sauce
1-2 tablespoons white wine vinegar
2 egg yolks
Pinch of cayenne pepper
Salt and pepper to taste
50-125g/2-4 oz /1/4-1/2 cup butter

Place the vinegar, egg yolks and seasonings in the top half of a double boiler, then whisk, with a balloon whisk, over hot water until the liquid begins to thicken. Cut the butter into small pieces and add it one piece at a time, allowing it to melt before whisking in the next. Do not let it come to the boil as it will curdle. Serve as sauce for salmon or green vegetables.

Italian Bread Salad

8 plum tomatoes, chopped
8 tablespoons extra-virgin olive oil
About 250g/8 oz/2 cups stale bread pieces
3 tablespoons water
1 garlic clove, finely chopped
2 tablespoons red wine vinegar
3 anchovy fillets, rinsed and finely chopped
Pinch of soft brown sugar
1425g/15 oz can white haricot (navy or Great Northern) beans in salt water, drained
3 teaspoons capers
2 tablespoons torn basil leaves
12 oz /350g canned tuna, drained
Salt and freshly ground black pepper

Season the tomatoes with salt and pepper and sprinkle them with one tablespoon of olive oil. Set aside. Toss the bread in a bowl with the water, three tablespoons of olive oil, garlic and salt and pepper to taste. Transfer the bread mixture to a frying pan and fry, turning constantly, for 5-8 minutes until the bread has a golden toasted colour.

In a blender, make the dressing, combining the remaining four tablespoons of olive oil with the vinegar, anchovy fillets and sugar and whisk for two minutes. In a serving bowl, place tomatoes, bread, white beans, capers, basil and tuna. Gently stir with a fork, letting the tuna break up into bite-sized pieces. Transfer the mixture to a serving bowl, sprinkle with the dressing, toss lightly and serve.

Horseradish Sauce

1 tablespoon white wine vinegar
2 tablespoons grated horseradish
2 teaspoons lemon juice
1/2 teaspoon Dijon mustard
125 ml /4 fl oz/1/2 cup double (heavy) cream
Pinch of sugar
Salt and pepper to taste

Put all the ingredients into a blender and blend until the cream has thickened. Serve with roast beef.

As wine is to Europe, rice is to Asia, and vinegar is the gastronomic transformation of both. The staple ingredient of Asia's diet, rice, has been cultivated for thousands of years; during that time, it has not only been used as a food, at one time in Japan it even became a currency.

History dates the origin of rice vinegar to the fourth century when China introduced it to Japan, neither country at the time realizing just how essential it would become to Japan. Since then, fermented rice vinegar has become a staple culinary ingredient in Japan.

China, Japan and Korea all produce varieties of rice vinegar, ranging in colour from clear through to black, all of them with a mellow, sweet flavour – thanks to the use of glutinous rice for the fermentation process. In Japan white rice vinegar, known as Komezu, is similar in colour to European vinegars. It is clear or pale gold in tone but the flavour is milder and it has a less acidic taste.

There is sometimes confusion between rice vinegar and rice wine vinegar – they are by no means the same thing. Rice wine vinegar is actually created by adding vinegar to the lees or dregs of rice wine. Sake and mirin are examples of rice wine vinegar.

China's black vinegar has a similar flavour and colour to Worcester sauce. It is extremely rich in amino acids. Predominant in southern China, the most popular version is Chinkiang, named after the province where it is made. Known never to spoil, this vinegar contains sixteen more amino acids than white rice vinegar and forty-three more than cider vinegar. A black vinegar is also made in Japan which, when mixed with water, is fast becoming popular as a health drink. Red vinegar is made by fermenting red yeast rice with a mould whose Latin name is Monascus purpureus. Red vinegar is used in both China and Japan.

Korean rice vinegar is made from unpolished rice. The flavour resembles a more acidic version of cider vinegar. Buddhists have a long association with Korean vinegar, particularly its health benefits, and it is said to promote a healthy heart.

The development of vinegar as a beauty aid is down to the belief that vinegar promotes healthier, more youthful skin. Vinegar increases the potency of vitamin C in the body thereby improving the complexion. This is widely known, leading to its adoption by the Japanese cosmetic industry in particular.

Rice vinegar's health benefits include improving the circulation, countering fatigue and assisting weight loss. It is being touted as a health drink in Japan. In Yokohama, there are shops selling the vinegar drink with staff acting as vinegar 'sommeliers' to encourage sales. The majority of the customers are women.

Making Process

Most rice vinegars are made from glutinous rice which gives the vinegar a sweet taste. Black vinegar is sometimes also made from sorghum or millet, and red rice vinegar uses rice fermented with a specific bacterial mould to develop its flavour. In all cases, the principle remains the same – the starch in the rice is allowed to convert to sugar, and then the sugar to create vinegar by acetic fermentation.

Originally, rice vinegar was made from cooking the rice in water, then introducing a wild yeast before allowing the sugar to ferment in each grain. Naturally brewed vinegar using this traditional method would then be stored for two to three years to further enhance the flavour. Commercial production speeds up the process, starting with alcohol and adding sugar and yeast.

For Japanese rice vinegar, the process commences with grinding the rice then steaming it in mesh baskets and mixing it with a yeast fungus. In the first few days, the chemical processes in the rice will

How To Use

All these vinegars are used in recipes of Asian origin. Rice vinegar preserves food longer and removes bitterness from vegetables, making it excellent for pickling.

Sushi – sushi wouldn't be sushi without Japanese white vinegar, nor would vinegared salads taste quite the same.

Sweet and Sour – Chinese white vinegar is used extensively in sweet and sour dishes.

Seafood – red vinegar works well with seafood, noodles and soups, and as a dipping sauce.

Stir-fries – black vinegar is used for stir-fries and braising, and as a condiment to be served at the table.

create hydrolytic enzymes, essential for the following stages. The mixture is then transferred to clay pots, submerged in water with added yeast and acetobacter – the vinegar bacteria.

Over the next six months, the hydrolytic enzymes convert the starch already present in the rice into fermenting sugars. The mixture is regularly stirred and, for centuries, the process across Asian countries has been to add specially selected microbial strains that can exist together, creating a mixed culture releasing complex flavours.

The main difference from European vinegar production is the outdoors effect. The vinegar is exposed to oxygen but in the open air, which makes it subject to the fluctuating temperature variations of day and night to increase the aerobic reaction.

Recipes

A visit to your local Asian grocery store will show you what a large selection of vinegars are available. With these recipes, you can start your own dim sum house!

Shrimp Relish
125 ml/4 fl oz/1/2 cup peanut oil
15 garlic cloves, finely chopped (minced)
5 bird's eye chillies, seeded and finely chopped
1 cm/1/2 inch dried shrimp paste (blachen)
250g/8 oz/2 cups dried prawns (shrimp)
125 ml/4 fl oz/1/2 cup sesame oil
50g/2 oz/1 cup chopped dried spring onions (scallions)
125 ml/4 fl oz/1/2 cup Chinese red vinegar
2 teaspoons Thai or Vietnamese fish sauce

Heat the peanut oil and stir-fry the garlic, chilli and shrimp paste until the garlic softens. Then allow to cool. Combine the dried prawns with the sesame oil.

Stir in the dried spring onions and the chilli-and-garlic mixture. Add the vinegar and fish sauce.

Seal in an airtight jar. Serve as an accompaniment to savoury dishes.

How To Make Sushi Rice

175g uncooked short-grain rice (or sushi rice)
225 ml /8 fl oz/1 cup cold water
2.5-5cm /1-2-inch strip of dried kelp (nori)

For the sushi vinegar:
1 1/2 tablespoons rice vinegar
1 tablespoon caster (superfine) sugar
1/2 teaspoon salt

Rinse the rice until the water runs clear and leave to drain for at least 30 minutes. The rice grains will swell with the moisture.

Put the rice, water and kelp in a pan and bring to the boil, removing the kelp just before the water boils. Cover the pan and simmer for about 10 minutes. Then remove the lid and cover the pan with a folded teatowel, allowing it to cool for 10 minutes. Mix the sushi vinegar ingredients together and pour into a saucepan. Place over a low heat until the sugar dissolves. Remove from the heat and pour into a bowl placed in cold water. This will stop the vinegar from fermenting further.

Spoon the rice into a bowl, spreading it out evenly. Use a wooden rice paddle to cut through the rice, side to side and top to bottom in a continuous movement. Make sure not to mash or stir the rice. As you do this, gradually add the sushi vinegar. The rice should be cool after 10 minutes and can then be served.

Chinese Dumpling Dipping Sauce

4 tablespoons light soy sauce
1 tablespoon sesame oil
1 tablespoon red rice vinegar
2 garlic cloves, chopped (minced)

Mix ingredients together and serve with fresh dumplings.

Flavoured vinegars use a wide range of herbs and spices to create amazing variations and are extremely simple to make for the everyday gourmet.

Tarragon vinegar is the leader in this field, closely followed by garlic, mint and hot chillies, though it seems that many herbs, spices and even flowers can be used. Malt, balsamic and wine vinegars have been added to food over the years to enhance flavours. But now the individual has the opportunity to experiment, mixing and creating unique flavours, employing them in personalized dishes to

Immersing flowers in vinegar will provide unusual and delicately-flavoured vinegars. Always use those that are guaranteed pesticide-free:

- Nasturtiums taste peppery
- Carnation petals are sweet
- Pansies will give an earthy flavour
- The flowers of a young dandelion are sweet to the taste
- Lavender offers a sweet taste and floral aroma

create distinctive aromas and secret recipes. With a proper knowledge of the different types of vinegar available and an understanding of the herbs and spices that can be complemented by sweet, bitter or sour vinegars, your kitchen can become a testing ground for investigative research – who knows, you could even make money from your creations!

Entrepreneurs have recognized this opportunity by producing flavoured vinegars for sale as edible gifts, usually complemented with bottles of flavoured oils. The bottles are quite decorative with highly visible and often whole chillies or sprigs of herbs immersed in the liquid.

The colour is dependent on the added ingredients but usually the vinegar appears as a golden liquid with the herbs prominently displayed. Homemade flavoured vinegars make excellent Christmas gifts, particularly if a few secret recipe ideas are included.

The individual has the opportunity to experiment, mixing and creating unique flavours

The main thing to remember when using herbs and spices is the need to slightly crush them

Making Process

Creating your own flavoured vinegar is simplicity itself and allows you to make whatever your heart desires. White vinegar is often used as the base, since its clarity and high acid content will complement the variety of added ingredients, but wine and apple cider vinegars are also frequently used and Asian vinegars offer a different range of flavours.

Herbs or spices are frequently immersed whole in vinegar. The main thing to remember when using herbs and spices is the need to slightly crush them, known as bruising, to allow the

flavour to slowly disperse. They can be chopped but there is debate as to whether this prevents the depth of flavour from building slowly.

The vinegar is simmered in a pan before being poured over the bruised herbs – some recipes state the liquid should never be boiled as it can make the vinegar too acidic. The purpose of heating the vinegar and then pouring it on the herbs or spices is to allow the initial release of a burst of flavour, before it mellows and is enhanced over time.

How To Use

Flavoured vinegar can be used in the same way as most other vinegars are – drizzled over vegetables, used as a dressing or as a base for sauces. You can swap ingredients in recipes, using flavoured vinegar with chilli vinegar, for example.

Lavender vinegar is also used for household cleaning and may be the first-ever fragrant disinfectant thanks to its pleasant smell.

Recipes

The recipes featured here will give you an idea of how to create your own flavoured vinegars, but feel free to experiment on your own. These recipes will make one 1 litre/1 3/4-pint/1-quart bottle that can be stored for up to two years. Always be sure to use clean, sterilized containers. Also included here is a favourite way of using tarragon vinegar – in classic Bearnaise Sauce.

Chilli Vinegar

Stand back when you pour in the heated vinegar because the aroma can pack quite an eye-watering punch. Finely chop 20 bird's eye chilli peppers and place in a bottle. Heat 500 ml/16 fl oz/2 cups of your chosen vinegar and pour it over the chillies. Let the open bottle stand for two weeks, shaking it once a day. In another bottle, place two or three whole chillies on a wooden skewer and put into the bottle. Strain the chilli from the liquid and pour into the bottle with the skewered chillies before corking.

Herb Vinegar

The same process can be used with any variety of herbs, including oregano, basil, chives, mint, rosemary, thyme and mixtures of any of the above. Work on the principle of one cup of herbs for every two cups of vinegar (cider vinegar is frequently used with herb vinegar) and ensure the herbs are bruised just prior to pouring the vinegar over them. Be sure to let the open bottle or jar stand in the sun to maximize the vinegar's flavour.

Garlic Vinegar

Using 30 garlic cloves, peel each one and either crush or chop them. A blender can be used but it may chop the garlic too finely, so it is best to chop it by hand. Place the garlic in a bottle. Heat 500 ml/16 fl oz/2 cups white vinegar, allow it to simmer for two minutes, just below the boil, then pour the vinegar over the garlic. Let the open bottle stand for two weeks, shaking it two or three times each day. Strain the garlic from the liquid and pour the liquid into a new clean bottle. Seal with a clean cork.

Horseradish Vinegar

Mix 7-15g/ 1/2-1 oz grated horseradish, 7g /1/2 oz finely chopped (minced) shallot and 7g/1/2 oz paprika. Add to one pint of vinegar. Let stand 7-10 days. Strain and then bottle.

Bearnaise Sauce

2 egg yolks
1-2 tablespoons tarragon vinegar, to taste
1 teaspoon chopped (minced) parsley
Pinch of cayenne pepper
30-60g/2-4 oz butter
Salt and pepper to taste

Place the egg yolks, seasonings and vinegar in the top pan of a double boiler. Bring the water in the lower pan to the boil,

whisking until the sauce begins to thicken. Gradually add small pieces of the butter, whisking in each piece as it melts before adding the next.

Do not let the mixture boil or it will curdle. Continue whisking until the required consistency is reached. Serve with steak.

While fruit vinegars have been in existence for over 10,000 years in some form or other, new varieties are becoming increasingly popular in modern cuisine.

fermented sugars in the juices are extremely concentrated and syrupy, depending on the type of vinegar used as the base, and the flavours are unique and mouth-watering. The latest trend is to dilute fruit vinegars with water to create a pleasant and refreshing drink, with health benefits an added bonus.

Create exotic flavours by using fruits such as mango, blackberry, pineapple, strawberry, gooseberry, guava or blood orange. All provide a unique sweetness and acetic tang. Fruits can also be combined to complement each other and mixed with a variety of standard vinegars – the variations are endless.

The variety of colour and taste of this style of vinegar results directly from the fruit used – the flavour can often resemble jam but with the refreshingly sour aftertaste of vinegar. The

Making Home-Made Vinegars

Home-made or gourmet vinegars can be created in many ways. As some vinegars are made from wine, fruit wines such as blackberry wine or raspberry wine – all make wonderful fruit vinegars. The home-made versions of these vinegars are somewhat simpler, offering a different flavour to those made commercially.

For apple cider vinegar, the fruit is steeped in water and allowed to stand to bring out the juices. The liquid is then strained and reserved while the fruit pulp is discarded. New fruit is added to the liquid, allowed to stand and the process is repeated. The liquid is finally strained once more and sugar is added and dissolved. The liquid is then allowed to stand in the open air until it becomes vinegar.

There is an even simpler process, however, for making flavoured vinegars – infusing your desired fruit in your chosen vinegar, whether that is sherry, white wine or cider. After all, experimenting is half the fun.

Fruit vinegars start with wonderful colours but eventually caramelize (turn brown) over time. Sometimes they turn cloudy, which is far from desirable.

To restore the colour, beat two egg whites with a little of the vinegar until it becomes frothy. Gradually add the egg whites to the cloudy vinegar, stirring well. Let the bottle stand for a week and the sediment will fall to the bottom. Siphon off the clear liquid into a new bottle.

Even if fruit vinegar turns brown, the acid content of vinegar will never allow it to spoil – in fact the flavour will improve!

How To Use

Refreshing drinks – the health benefits offered by vinegar have the potential to be the next 'big thing' in health drinks, fruit vinegars being as delicious and refreshing as they are.

Dressing – fruit vinegars make excellent green salad dressings or they can be drizzled over fruit salads or fruit preserves.

Recipes

Here are a few suggestions of how to make your own fruit vinegars, plus a selection of recipes to use them in.

Blueberry Vinegar
1.25 l/2 1/2 pints/5 cups cider vinegar
1 kilo/2 1/4 lb blueberries

Boil the vinegar rapidly for two minutes. Remove from heat and allow to cool. Wash and drain the blueberries, then place in blender and grind for two to three minutes or until crushed.

Transfer the blueberries to a large jar then pour the cooled vinegar over them. Cover with muslin (cheesecloth), held in place with a rubber band or twine, and leave in a warm place for one month. Then strain through a clean filter (either muslin (cheesecloth) or a coffee filter will do) to strain the sediment and fruit. Finally, pour the liquid into sterilized bottles and seal.

Summer Refresher

1 tablespoon strawberry vinegar
1 teaspoon sugar
18 fl oz/500 ml/2 cups soda water (club soda)
18 fl oz/500 ml/2 cups ginger ale

Mix the ingredients together and serve with ice. Don't tell your guests they are drinking vinegar but watch their reaction when you tell them afterwards.

Raspberry Vinegar Dressing

2 tablespoons sour cream
125 ml/4 fl oz/1/2 cup raspberry vinegar
60 ml/2 fl oz/1/4 cup olive oil
1 tablespoon chopped (minced) chives
Salt and pepper to taste

Place sour cream in a bowl and stir in vinegar, oil and chives. Stir until smooth, adding salt and pepper to taste. Serve with a green salad.

Cranberry Sage Vinegar

30g/2 oz/1/4 cup fresh cranberries
1.25 litres/2 1/8 pints/5 cups apple cider vinegar
3 tablespoons white sugar
2 teaspoons dried sage

Thread the cranberries on to thin wooden skewers.

Combine the vinegar and sugar in a saucepan and simmer until the sugar dissolves, ensuring the liquid does not boil. Once the sugar dissolves, place the base of the saucepan in cold water to arrest the cooking process and allow the liquid to cool.

Place the sage and cranberries in a clean bottle. Fill the bottle with the cooled vinegar and allow it to settle for an hour. Then seal the bottle and let it stand for at least two weeks before use.

The common belief is that anything made from sugar cane must be as sweet as sugar itself but this is not the case with cane vinegar.

Vinegar made from crushed sugar cane was originally known as sukan iloko and comes from the Ilocos region of the Philippines. It is now made throughout the country and is even produced in Japan, France and North America.

The taste of cane vinegar is not dissimilar to that of rice vinegar but this vinegar does not retain any of the sweet taste of sugar cane because it holds no residual sugars. It is usually golden in colour but can range from dark yellow to toffee brown, and has a mellow, fresh taste.

Making Cane Vinegar

Sugar cane growing regions of the Philippines often have excess sugar cane that for many reasons is unsuitable for sugar production. To make vinegar, the cane is washed and crushed to extract the juice, which is then collected in earthen jars.

The juice is brought to a high temperature either through boiling or being left standing for a day in the sun. Fresh yeast is added, stirred into the mixture with wooden spoons and, over the following couple of days, impurities rise to the surface. These are skimmed off, resulting in the production of a clear, amber liquid.

The liquid is left for more days to ferment and turn to alcohol, in this case without exposure to air. The yeast is drawn off and 'mother of vinegar' is added. The mixture is stirred once a day until the required vinegar strength is achieved.

Recipes

Sugar Cane Vinegar Squid

1 medium squid
75 ml/2 1/2 fl oz/1/3 cup sugar cane vinegar
6 garlic cloves, finely chopped (minced)
50 ml/2 fl oz/1/4 cup soy sauce
125 ml/4 fl oz/1/2 cup water
1/2 teaspoon black pepper
2 tablespoons vegetable oil
1 medium onion, sliced
1 can diced tomatoes

Rinse the squid and dry it with paper towels. Separate the tentacles and cut the body into 2 cm / 3/4 inch-wide rings. Pour the vinegar into a saucepan and add the garlic, soy sauce, water and pepper and bring to the boil; boil for one minute. Add the squid and cook over high heat, stirring the mixture until the squid becomes opaque.

Remove from the heat, draining the liquid into a bowl, and allow the squid to cool. Sauté the onion until lightly browned, then add the tomatoes. Then bring to the boil, stirring, until the liquid reduces and becomes syrupy, about five minutes. Add the squid liquid and bring back to the boil; this time let the liquid reduce by half. Stir in the squid and simmer for two minutes. Serve with rice and steamed bok choy.

How To Use

Meats and sauces – excellent for teriyaki and peppery sauces, cane vinegar complements any spicy dish and is particularly good with seafood recipes. Cane vinegar is also used in cakes and soufflés.

Coconut vinegar is surprisingly not made from the coconut, that exceptionally versatile fruit, but from the sap of the coconut palm.

It is extremely popular in the Philippines and may yet take the world by storm as the organic version comes to market.

Coconut vinegar is known as tuba and is similar to coconut water, the liquid found inside a coconut. It contains essential vitamins and minerals such as beta-carotene, calcium, magnesium, potassium, iron, sodium and phosphorous. The colour of the vinegar starts as cloudy white before changing to light yellow and eventually to brown as

How To Use

Jack of all trades – coconut vinegar is frequently used in Filipino dishes. It also works well in dips, salad dressings and mayonnaise. It can replace lemon juice and is an excellent substitute for salt in foods.

Digestion – the high potassium and trace element content makes the vinegar a good aid to digestion.

it matures. Some commercial vinegars are made with added yeast and sugar. The 'mother of vinegar' occurs naturally in the liquid, so it will ferment without additives in weeks. Commercially produced vinegar is then heated to pasteurize it.

Making Coconut Vinegar

Tuba collectors are masters of the technique of climbing coconut palms, since they need to get right to the top. The tuba sap lives in the spadix, the thick branch from which the plant flowers, which is rich in sap to feed the growing coconuts. The collector must climb to the top of the tree to reach the spadix, sit, cut the stem and hang a vessel from the tree, allowing the sap to run into it. And this is the job of all jobs – every day the tuba collector has to travel from palmtop to palmtop, gathering sap from each palm. Once collected, the natural fermentation process takes over 45-60 days to ferment the tuba sap into vinegar, which can be left unfiltered and unheated for the final product.

Recipes

Coconut Vinegar Cream
16 fl oz/500 ml/2 cups sour cream
250 ml/8 fl oz/1 cup coconut cream
250 ml/8 fl oz/1 cup coconut vinegar
Salt and pepper to taste

Combine the ingredients, adding more vinegar until you have the required consistency. You can add other herbs or garlic, even some chilli powder.

Coconut Vinegar Vinaigrette
75 ml/2 1/2 fl oz/1/3 cup sesame oil
2 tablespoons coconut vinegar
3 garlic cloves, finely chopped (minced)
2 teaspoons grated fresh ginger
1 teaspoon sesame seeds
2 spring onions (scallions), green parts only, chopped
Salt and pepper to taste

Mix all ingredients in a glass jar and shake well. Used as a salad dressing, coconut vinegar vinaigrette is particularly good when poured over cabbage salads.

It's true, it seems, that you can turn almost anything into vinegar, as long as there is sugar and starch, grain or fruit – even vegetables can become vinegar.

Nowadays, almost any food can be purchased ready-made, but here are some traditional vinegars which are hard to come by outside their native land and are mainly home-made.

Date Vinegar

Similar to fruit vinegars, date vinegar is produced throughout the Middle East, Africa, India and Asia. Dates have been the staple diet of the inhabitants of arid lands

and deserts for thousands of years because of their health benefits – protein, copper, sulphur, iron, magnesium and fluoric acid are all found in the fruit. Countries such as Morocco, Iran and Lebanon all use date vinegar in their food. Organic date vinegar could one day offer as many benefits as organic apple cider vinegar. The colour is quite dark, with an aroma of sweet dates.

Honey Vinegar

Although an expensive rarity, honey vinegar is finding its place in Italy and France. The scarcity of this vinegar is due to its cost, because a significant supply of honey can make the process expensive – compare the cost of one apple against the same quantity of honey and you can see the problem.

The healing properties of honey combined with vinegar make it an exceptional medicine, as honey increases the therapeutic benefits offered by vinegar, speeding its assimilation into the body. The colour of honey vinegar depends on the

The vinegar flavour is very much dependent upon the type of beer used

initial honey used. Darker honeys will ferment faster than lighter versions. The final product is rich tasting but still has that distinctive vinegar tang.

Beer Vinegar

As noted in the section about malt vinegar, brewers often create a very good vinegar by default. Producers of beer have discovered this beneficial by-product and, though not commonly used worldwide, German, Austrian and Dutch manufacturers have brought beer vinegar on to the market.

The vinegar flavour is very much dependent upon the type of beer used, particularly with regards to its taste. Usually a warm dark brown, beer vinegar has a flavour which is definitively malty.

There is an irony in the fact that time is the key to vinegar, both in its history and production, and yet the taste is sharp and not one to savour for too long. Traditional methods devote an extraordinary length of time to creating the best vinegars available.

Nowadays, when the pace of everything else is quickening, this liquid is allowed the luxury of developing its flavour and complexity over many months and years.

Vinegar is still produced the traditional way and, from this, industrial processes have emerged and developed, allowing many types and variations of vinegar to be produced around the world. The benefit of modern technology is that it allows greater accessibility for the consumer, who is able to purchase almost any type of vinegar needed.

But like all commercial products, price is a factor – the longer the vinegar has taken to make, the higher the cost. The longer the maturing time, in theory, the better the vinegar should taste. Many chefs will argue the same flavour cannot be extracted from an industrially made vinegar as can be achieved from a traditionally made version. But depending on the purpose, the requirement may be merely for a vinegar that has been produced on an industrial scale.

The three methods used for vinegar production are the generator or trickling method, the submerged fermentation method and the Orleans traditional method.

The same flavour cannot be extracted from an industrially made vinegar as can be achieved from a traditionally made one

The Generator Method

Also known as the trickling method, this process allows alcohol to slowly trickle from the top of the vat across vinegar-moistened wood shavings (some manufacturers also use grape pulp or charcoal). The vats may be made from wood or stainless steel. Holes in the sides and bottom of the vat allow air compressors to continually blow oxygen through the vat to aerate the vinegar.

Over a period of time, ranging anything from days to weeks, the alcohol turns into vinegar, which eventually permeates down to the bottom of the vat. The vinegar is then drawn off and stored. Its acetic acid level at this stage is quite high and the liquid needs to be diluted with water to reduce it to 5%. This method is normally used to make distilled vinegar.

The next stage in the distillation process is to boil the liquid, from which a vapour is collected into a condenser. This vapour then turns back into a liquid, which is subsequently bottled and ends up on the supermarket shelf as distilled vinegar.

The Submerged Fermentation Method

Imagine a steel tank filled with alcohol and pumped with oxygen at the temperature of a warm summer day, and you have the basics of the submerged fermentation method.

Primarily used to produce wine vinegars, this process was developed in the 1950s, using tanks called acetators. The wine is kept at a temperature of between 26-38°C (79-100°F) while nutrients are pumped into the mixture.

These nutrients work with the heat and oxygen, creating acetobacters, and the wine turns into vinegar within a very short space of time. The vinegar is then washed to remove sediment and diluted with water to reach the appropriate acetic acid level.

Pasteur's discoveries are believed to have had a negative effect on the flavour of vinegar

Air is the key to this process – exposing the wine to the air creates vinegar, so being able to maximize the air flow provides a faster process for vinegar creation. While Pasteur's discoveries of micro-organisms revolutionized vinegar production, some would say it has had a detrimental effect on flavour.

Most industrial vinegar companies have emergency generators in place for fear of power cuts – loss of power could kill the acetobacter cultures in seconds, destroying thousands of litres of vinegar.

The Orleans Method

Developed in the town of Orleans in the Loire Valley, France, this process uses time to mature the flavours in vinegar. During the Middle Ages, Orleans was a river port and many cargoes reached the town on their way to other regions in France.

One of the key industries of the time was wine-making and many barrels were shipped from Orleans along the network of rivers and canals. Fortunately for the town of Orleans, many a barrel of wine spoiled due to exposure to heat and poor storage facilities. Barrels were left exposed to the sun at the quayside, but when the wine became undrinkable, the town of Orleans saw a very real opportunity.

Sensing that the enormous supply could result in popular demand, the town became one of the largest vinegar-producing sites, using the barrels of spoiled claret and other wines. With time, an industry was created, specializing in the wonderful flavours of wine vinegar. The stranded wines were of many types, including some extremely expensive vintages – the folk of Orleans must have rubbed their hands with glee, as vintage wine resulted in vintage vinegar. The township thrived, with hundreds of vinegar production factories being set up, in which the vinegar was stored for anywhere between six months and many, many years.

The original Orleans process involves using the same wooden barrels in which the wine is fermented or transferring the wine into a prepared barrel. In either case, the barrel is laid on its side and holes drilled in the top and sides, above the level of the vinegar. These holes allow air to enter the barrel. They are loosely corked but not fully sealed, to allow oxygen to enter.

As contamination, in the form of flying insects or other matter, would spell disaster for the vinegar, special netting is placed over the holes and this is carefully inspected daily. 'Mother of vinegar' is funnelled carefully through the holes so that it lies on top of the alcohol. The barrel is left for many months at a warm and consistent temperature, gradually turning the wine alcohol into vinegar.

When the maker is finally happy with the flavour of the vinegar, it is siphoned off into another barrel and stored again to allow the complexity of flavours to develop even further. The vinegar is then bottled and sold. In the case of white wine vinegar, herbs are added and the vinegar is left to mature for several months more. For example, tarragon vinegar was, and still is, a key product made from wine vinegar; it has been used widely in French cooking and its popularity

has now spread around the world.

A sour note enters here, though. Louis Pasteur's discovery of micro-organisms dramatically decreased production time.

This revolution in vinegar creation resulted in the near-demise of the Orleans process and eventually led to a sharp decrease in production in the area.

However, producers in Orleans still use the traditional method to create the very best vintage wine vinegars.

'Mother Of Vinegar'

While any description of vinegar-making can appear complex and time-consuming, making your own vinegar at home is not a difficult process. In order to do it successfully, your first step is to make your own 'mother'.

Essentially, 'mother of vinegar' is a culture made from yeast and acetic acid bacteria which, when mixed with alcohol such as wine, or with unfermented sugary juice such as apple juice or cane juice, helps to ferment the liquid. Oxygen then assists in turning it into acetic acid and thus vinegar.

These days, making your own 'mother' is a simple process, mainly because it is widely available commercially. The scum at the bottom of an unfiltered, unpasteurized bottle of vinegar is the remnants of the 'mother'.

While most of us today would steer away from consuming the rather unprepossessing-looking culture, it has health benefits and is completely harmless. It should be added to the new liquid in a ratio of 1:4. The higher the sugar content of your liquid, the better your vinegar will be.

To start from scratch, place in a large, clean jar 500 ml/16 fl oz/2 cups vinegar and 500 ml/16 fl oz/2 cups wine, cider or fruit juice, ensuring

that, if you use fruit juice, you use an organic, unfiltered product (some manufacturers introduce preservatives into fruit juice which can inhibit the bacterial reaction in vinegar).

Cover the jar with a piece of cheesecloth or other porous fabric so that air can still enter the jar but insects will be prevented from stopping by for a visit (and they will come calling). Place the jar in a warm place, such as an airing cupboard, and leave it for two weeks – a scum will develop across the top of the liquid. This is the 'mother', the acetobacter bacteria essential to creating vinegar.

Once you have started the culture of the 'mother', you should continue to feed it further by adding more alcohol at least once a month to allow it to thrive.

To create vinegar, skim the 'mother' from the top of the fluid. Pour fresh wine or juice into a new container and add the mother, ensuring that it stays on top of the liquid. Cover the container with a porous fabric that will allow oxygen to enter.

It is important not to let the 'mother of vinegar' sink to the bottom of the liquid as it needs oxygen to create the acetic acid reaction. This is bound to happen eventually, but at this stage of the vinegar-making process, you need to keep the mother at the top, so if you want to add more fresh alcohol or juices, pour the liquid in gradually, trickling it down the side of the container.

Keep the vinegar mixture in a warm place. Some would argue that a dark place will allow the mixture to mature better and light can sometimes affect the fermentation processes that are occurring. It is up to you how long you leave your vinegar to stand, but warmth is the key element. At first, aim to store it for a month and taste the vinegar weekly so you can understand how it progresses through to maturity, recording its development for reference purposes.

The flavour of your home-made vinegar will be quite strong, but it is easy to dilute it with water until you achieve your preferred flavour. Remember also that vinegar involves time, and aging the vinegar over weeks or months is the best way to ensure that the complexity of flavours will develop.

When you are finally happy with the taste, pour the vinegar through a paper filter into a clean, sterile glass bottle. Cork the bottle – don't use metal caps as they will disintegrate – and pour a wax seal around the top to guarantee that no further air will enter the bottle. It is possible to pasteurize the vinegar but this tends to diminish the complexity of flavours you have created. It is best to draw off only as much as you need from the original starter – you can always go back for more.

Understanding Acetic Acid

Shop-bought vinegars have an acetic acid content of 4-6%. Home-made vinegar may have an acid level in excess of this range, which will, in turn, affect consumption and overall flavour. To discover the strength of your vinegar, you will require a titration kit, available from a wine-making supplier. Using a pH tester will help determine the strength of the vinegar, which should not exceed a pH of 7.

Another tried and tested method, though not quite as accurate, is to test it using bicarbonate of soda (baking soda) and cabbage water. Boil 250 ml/8 fl oz/1 cup red cabbage in water until the water turns a deep purple colour. Discard the cabbage and save the water. In a separate glass of water, dissolve two teaspoons of bicarbonate of soda – this is your soda water. To create your test controls, fill two glasses with plain water. Label one glass 'control' and the other 'experiment'. To both of these glasses, add two tablespoons cabbage water. Add ten drops of

commercial vinegar, preferably plain white vinegar, to the control glass, and then 20 drops of your soda water, stirring with a plastic spoon until the water turns blue. The acetic acid of commercial vinegar should be labelled as being 5%, which is what you are aiming for with yours.

To the experiment glass, add seven drops of your own home-made vinegar then add drops of soda water, counting drops as you go, until the water turns the same shade of blue as the control glass. The two levels of acetic acid should then be equal in both glasses. Divide the total number of each drop of soda water in the experiment glass by four and this will give you the percentage of your vinegar's acidity.

For example, if it took 40 drops of soda water to turn your vinegar blue, divide the 40 by four – the acetic acid content of your vinegar is 10%. This would be far too high for human consumption and shows that the vinegar needs to be diluted with water.

The acetic acid of commercial vinegar should be labelled as being 5%, which is what you are aiming for with your own vinegar

What can go wrong

The vinegar smells bad

Give the vinegar some time to develop, it will improve as it matures further. If, however, it still smells bad after a month, the mixture may not have received enough oxygen. This would happen if the cloth covering is too thick or there is not enough air in the place where the vinegar was stored.

How to cure it

Pour the vinegar from one container to another a couple of times in a day to let oxygen in. Leave it to stand for a few more days, ensuring the cloth covering allows oxygenation. Taste it in about a week and it should have improved.

Vinegar is too weak

It may have been too heavily diluted with water or the acetic acid has converted further to carbonic acid and water.

How to cure it

Add more alcohol so that any remaining vinegar can commence its work again. Vinegar contains live bacteria, so to maintain its strength it needs to be fed.

Nothing appears to have happened

Sulphites may be present in your original liquid. Sulphites work as a preservative and stop the vinegar reaction. Some wine and fruit juice producers include sulphite in the final product to ensure that it doesn't spoil.

How to cure it

Dilute the vinegar with water to try to destabilize the preservative. If this doesn't work, unfortunately you will have to start again, this time making sure that the liquid contains no preservatives. Check the label on the bottle or otherwise aim for organic fruit juice and wines, which are sulphite-free.

Still nothing appears to be happening...

The bacteria may not be viable. This may occur because the 'mother' has not received enough oxygen or the mother may have sunk to the bottom of the liquid.

The solution

Try to bring the mother back to the surface, adding fresh alcohol. If this does not work, you will need to start again.

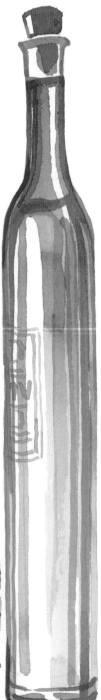

Variations on vinegar

Honey Vinegar

This vinegar is a popular natural folk remedy, but it is expensive and in short supply so make your own variation at home.

In a bowl, dissolve one sachet of yeast in warm water, allowing it to stand until it becomes frothy. Pour 2 litres/3 1/2 pints/8 cups of boiling water over 1 1/2 kg /3 lb 5 oz/6 2/3 cups of honey and stir until the honey dissolves. Spread the yeast on one side of a slice of toast and leave it, yeast side up, in the honey water for three weeks. Keep the container covered with a cheesecloth to ensure no foreign bodies get into the liquid.

After three weeks, remove the toast and strain the liquid into another bowl. There will be scum across the top which can be discarded. Let the liquid stand for another month, tasting it regularly until you are happy with the flavour. This will make a delicious vinegar, extremely good for fighting sore throats and colds in the winter time.

Wine Vinegar

Just as the ancients discovered, an open bottle of wine can easily turn into vinegar, especially if you leave it in the sunshine. You can speed your own wine vinegar-making process by adding some 'mother of vinegar' for a quicker result.

Place your wine in a large glass bowl with a little active vinegar. Let the wine sit, covered with cheesecloth, for a few weeks. The 'mother' will hasten the conversion into vinegar and you can keep ageing it in open bottles for as long as you like.

Apple Cider Vinegar

There are two ways of making apple cider vinegar, both of which have their uses. One uses the best home-grown apples you can find and the other uses the peelings, cores and any scraps of the fruit. In either case, the high sugar content in apples is the starting point for a great vinegar.

For the home-grown version, it is best if you can pick apples from your own tree but, if not, aim to find the very best organic apples. Wash the apples thoroughly and cut ten of them into quarters – you don't need to peel them or core them (but if you choose to, you can use them to make the other type of vinegar). Let them turn brown through exposure to air, then place them in a glass bowl and add water to cover. Place cheesecloth or other porous material over the bowl and leave for six months in a warm, dark place. Remember to avoid bright light, as this can interfere with the fermentation process.

After this time, you should find that a grey scum has formed over the liquid. Filter the liquid through a coffee filter and transfer what has now become cider to another, larger bowl. Leave it for another 4-6 weeks. The larger bowl will increase the density of oxygen available to the mixture and it, too, will still need to be covered with porous cloth to stop extraneous matter, such as insects, falling into it.

Using fruit scraps works on a similar principle except you use only cores and peelings. This mixture will thicken over a period of weeks, particularly if you continue to add new scraps and peelings every day or so, until a scum starts to form. Then stop and leave the mixture for a month, tasting it to determine its vinegar strength. When you are happy with the flavour, strain it through a filter and into a bottle.

Cleopatra knew about the beautifying effects of pickles when used on the skin. Christopher Columbus cheated scurvy thanks to storing pickles on his journeys across the sea – indeed, pickles and preserves hold their own special place in world history.

The first confirmed mention of vinegar being used for preserving food dates back to 2300 BCE in India, a country known for creating exotic-tasting pickles and chutneys, and archaeol-ogists claim that it was used in Mesopotamia. Records also show that the Romans fed pickles to their troops to increase their strength and Napoleon valued the power of the pickle for fortifying his armies.

Pickles still have their place in the modern world. Every Big Mac contains a pickled gherkin. Bearing that in mind, it's hardly surprising that the Americans are enthusiasts, consuming well over five million pounds (2,300,000 kg) of pickles per year. Not to be outdone, the British have honoured favourites, including the pickled onion, chutney and piccalilli – even Queen Elizabeth I had a penchant for these delightful flavours.

The purpose of pickling was and still is to maintain and preserve food that would otherwise spoil. Our ancestors did not have the luxury of refrigeration as a means of storing foods for winter or to tide them over poor harvests. When harvests were abundant, not allowing produce to go to waste was a key concern.

So pickling vegetables and preserving fruits became standard practices as such methods would keep the food edible and prevent the incursion of bacteria and food poisoning, which could even be fatal.

Preservation was achieved by dry-salting or covering with oil, sugar and, of course, vinegar; the acetic acid in vinegar maintains the pH balance of the food.

Using certain vinegar types with specific foods enhances the flavour and, when stored over a period of time, wonderful tastes can emerge. As we know, vinegar is produced all over the world – pickling and preserving are popular in many countries.

Currently, pickles and preserves are widely available in supermarkets and, fortunately for the consumer, they are still available in large quantities, despite the availability of fresh produce all year round. Unfortunately, the art of making preserves at home has become sadly neglected, though, thanks to the re-emergence of slow food cooking (a response to fast food), this trend may be reversed.

The art of pickling and preserving is to plan extensively for meals many, many months away. For instance, plums can be preserved for chutney in the autumn which will be devoured at Christmas dinner and green tomato pickle can be stored for three months before it is used to spice up curries or barbecued meats. Pickling can yield inspirational food using fresh, young vegetables and makes it possible to find new ways to use foods that are readily available. If you grow your own food, the ability to add longevity to your produce and keep it available in the pantry throughout the seasons makes the effort of pickling all the more worth-while.

How To Pickle

There are many ways of preserving food. Canned and bottled foods require the right tools and utensils to ensure the safety of the end product.

The favourite preserving jar is the Mason jar, a patented heavy glass jar developed by John Landis Mason in 1858, which is able to withstand the heat process of pickling. It was further developed with the introduction of metal lids in 1881 by Alfred Bernardin, producing what we know today as the standard Mason preserving jar.

It is possible to use other types and styles of jars and bottles but the key element is to ensure the seal will not allow air to seep into the preserve, keeping out the harmful bacteria. Other types of bottles and jars, not especially made for preserving, can be sealed with corks and wax which have been fully sterilized then heat-sealed.

Three canning techniques are used for pickling, all of which are specific to the type of pickle being made and also to the vegetables or fruits used. The length of storage time will also determine which method is used, as some pickles will keep for years, while others must be used in a matter of weeks.

The open-kettle method is used when the foods are cooked in an uncovered pot. The liquid is brought to the boil, creating its own form of sterilization, and, when at its highest temperature, the liquid and solids are poured into jars and sealed

immediately. To use this method, you need a steady hand, as the liquid may be scalding. The other equipment such as funnels, non-corrosive pans and temperature gauges have made this a popular process, particularly for making jams and preserves, because the food can be stored for years.

Hot-packed pickling is a similar method. The foods are blanched or cooked briefly then packed into jars. Vinegar is then brought to boiling point and poured directly over the food, then sealed immediately. This method works exceptionally well on most young vegetables, though not so well with tomatoes. The process of blanching also enhances the colour of the vegetables, creating a depth and vibrancy that makes them look particularly appetizing in the jar. This method is frequently used to preserve garden produce and make it accessible throughout the year, though in some cases the pickles should be consumed as soon as one month after making.

Vegetables and fruit can also be pickled straight from their natural raw state without cooking. For this to be successful, cleanliness is crucial for both jars and foods. Place raw foods into sterilized jars and cover completely with the preferred pickling liquid (vinegar, brine, syrup or sauce). As the liquid can also be added cold, it is essential that the jar is sealed immediately. Most foods pickled this way can only be stored for a few months.

The final element of pickling and preserving is to ensure the product is adequately sterilized. Even using germ-free jars and the cleanest vegetables, the space between the food and the lid can be a breeding-ground for bacteria, so the final sterilization process is essential.

The most common method is the vacuum heat-seal or water-bath process in which jars, already filled with pickles and sealed, are placed on a rack in a deep pan. Hot water is then added to cover the jars to a depth of 2.5-5cm/1-2 inches above the lids. The water should be hot, but not boiling, as some jars can crack if suddenly exposed to extreme temperatures. The water is then brought to boiling point, a temperature of 100°C (212°F), and then usually left for ten minutes to ensure any bacteria are killed.

The jars are then removed and left to cool on wire racks and it is during this process that a vacuum seal is created. If a preserving jar with a metal lid is used, the top will become concave in the centre if it is properly sealed. This seal ensures the jar is adequately sterilized and no bacteria should be able to breed.

A similar process to the vacuum seal is the use of steam heat, which is particularly useful if the foods might deteriorate from spending too long in boiling water. The following recipes will indicate which method is required. The jars should be placed on a wire rack in the pan or in a steamer,

Essential Equipment

Pans – these should be deep and non-corrosive

Racks – for placing inside the pans and on which to cool the jars; ensure that they are sturdy

Tongs – hot jars are difficult to lift out of water; tongs will make it easier

Funnels – aim for the jar not the kitchen table, particularly crucial when pouring hot pickles into jars

Thermometer – essential for testing the temperature

since it is essential that boiling water does not touch the jars. Covering the pan will turn it into a steam pressure cooker and the pickles should cook at high intensity for a very short period of time.

The last of the methods is for foods that soften if exposed to high temperatures, such as cucumbers. Low-temperature pasteurization uses the same principle as the vacuum heat-seal but maintains a temperature of 85°C (185°F) and does not allow it to rise further. The above processes have been tried and tested over many, many years and the rules of pickling, if followed correctly, should mean nothing ever goes wrong. That said, it is true that the more you pickle, the better you will become at it – and, like all cooking methods, defining your own style is half the fun.

What Can Go Wrong

The purpose of preserving is the safe storage of food and, to achieve this, cleanliness is king. With all your equipment, containers, seals and the food itself, it is essential they are hygienically prepared in order to avoid harmful bacteria or insects getting into pickles or preserves. There are many factors that can contribute to a poorly made or unsafe product, so strict attention must always be paid to temperature, level of acidity and processing times.

Containers

Carefully check your jars, seals and corks. These must be completely free of chips, nicks, cracks, stains or rust to guarantee hygiene and safety. When you have finished filling them with the pickle or preserve, run a cloth dipped in vinegar around the top of the jar and the seal to disinfect them.

Pans & Bowls

Vinegar will corrode reactive metal and will create unpleasant flavours and strange colorations. Use non-corrosive pans such as stainless steel and avoid copper, iron and brass. Plastic or wooden utensils are also advisable.

Sterilization

Ensure the containers you are using to store your preserves are completely sterile through boiling or oven-drying. To sterilize preserving jars, place your washed, clean jars in a pan, cover them with water and boil for a minimum of ten minutes. Do not transfer the jars into warm water immediately or instantly remove them from boiling water as the glass will break if it is subjected to

sudden extremes of temperature. Once the jars are ready, lift them out of the pan using a sterilized utensil and leave them to dry upside down on a clean cloth or drying rack. All rubber seals and corks should be subjected to the same procedure. If you are using muslin (cheesecloth) on which to stand the jars, pour boiling water through the fabric and allow to dry. To sterilize by oven drying, heat the oven to 160°C (325°F). Place your jars in the oven and keep them there for ten minutes. Allow them to cool slightly before filling.

Blanching

Ensure that any food you wish to use is always thoroughly cleaned before preparing. Spending more time cleaning in cold water will benefit the final product. When your food is ready for preparation, blanching is the next step as this will retain the colour of the food and also destroy any enzymes present, which over time will cause deterioration. Place the food into boiling water for two minutes then drain and transfer to ice water, to cease the cooking process instantly. Drain again, then start the recipe.

Foods

Ensure that you always use the freshest and barely ripe vegetables or fruits. The younger the foods, the crunchier they will be. They will also produce a better flavour. Sort through the foods carefully and discard any that are bruised or mouldy. If using fruits and vegetables from the garden, when possible try to finish the pickling process within 48 hours of harvesting, to ensure freshness. Try not to refrigerate foods before use, as cold temperatures can induce subsequent deterioration. Ensure you weigh foods carefully, as it is important to get the right balance between the food and the preserving liquid.

Salt

Salt has long been known as the other essential ingredient for preserves but it is important to use the right kind of salt when mixing it with vinegar. Normal table salt is usually iodized and this will create a reaction in preserved food. Some salts also contain anti-caking agents and these will turn the vinegar cloudy. Use a coarse salt, koshering salt or a salt specially manufactured for pickling salt as these will flavour the food without changing the colour or transparency of the liquid.

Sugar

Also used to flavour preserves; white granulated sugar is the most common but brown sugar adds a milder flavour. Some recipes also use honey but you need to be careful as some honeys can have strong flavours – what tastes great on your toast, when mixed with vegetables, fruits and vinegar, can create an unpleasant combination of flavours. And what may taste fine in the initial mixture can become disagreeable over time so the key to using sugar – and salt – is to stick to the amounts in the recipe.

Vinegar

Ensure your vinegar is 5% acetic acid strength. Stronger vinegar will give a tough texture to foods and weaker vinegar will create soft, slimy foods. Once you have the right level of acidity, keep it at full strength and, if you are unhappy with the

> Always ensure that you use the freshest and barely ripe vegetables. The younger the foods, the crunchier they will be

flavour, use sugar to address it, rather than diluting the liquid. If you are using a heat process for pickling, stick to the time recommended for boiling, as acetic acid will evaporate and the pickle will become soft. White vinegar is the most frequent pickling medium, as its transparency will enhance the brightness of the vegetable or fruit. You can also use apple cider vinegar or malt vinegar – it all depends on taste.

Recipes

Plum Chutney

1kg /2 1/4 lb large red plums, stoned (pitted) and halved
500g/1 lb 2 oz apples, cored and chopped
300g/10 1/2 oz red onions, finely chopped
2 garlic cloves, finely chopped (minced)
1 tablespoon fresh grated ginger root
1 cinnamon stick
1 teaspoon ground allspice
1 teaspoon ground cloves
3 bird's eye chillies, finely chopped (minced)
(or more if you really want to spice it up)
500g/1 lb 2 oz/2 cups light brown sugar
750 ml /1 1/4 pints/3 cups apple cider vinegar

Place all the ingredients in a large preserving pan and bring the mixture slowly to the boil, stirring to dissolve the sugar. Reduce the heat and let the mixture simmer for one hour or until the liquid starts to thicken. Stir continually as the liquid evaporates. Remove the pan from the heat and allow the mixture to cool briefly before bottling in sterilized jars.

Green Tomato Pickle

600 ml/1 pint/2 1/2 cups white vinegar
500g/1 lb/2 cups white sugar
50g/2 oz/1/4 cup dill seed
1 tablespoon mustard seed
1 tablespoon celery seed
1 tablespoon salt
1kg /2 1/4 lb green tomatoes, blanched then quartered
1 medium white onion, thinly sliced

Combine all the ingredients, except the tomatoes and onions, in a preserving pan and bring to the boil. Add the tomatoes and onions and simmer for 10 minutes. Pour into sterilized clamp-top jars and then vacuum seal with the heat or steam process. The pickles can be eaten within a month but, for better flavour, keep them for two to three months.

Pickled Onions

550g/1 lb 4 oz small white pickling onions
1/2 tablespoon salt
500 ml/18 fl oz/2 cups water
500 ml/18 fl oz/2 cups malt vinegar
2 teaspoons mustard seed
1 tablespoon sugar
1/2 teaspoon ground pepper

Peel the onions, place in a bowl and cover with salt. Leave for 12 hours. Drain the onions and place into prepared jars. Place the remaining ingredients in a pan and boil until the sugar has dissolved. Pour the mixture over the onions leaving a gap of 2 cm / 3/4 inch at the top of the jar. Weigh down the onions using a plate or pebble and seal them. They will be ready to eat within a month.

Bread & Butter Pickle

750g /1 lb 10 oz pickling cucumbers
625g/1 lb 6 oz white onions, sliced
375g /13 oz yellow bell peppers, sliced
3 tablespoons salt
1 litre /1 3/4 pints/4 cups white vinegar
500g /1 lb/2 cups white sugar
1 teaspoon ground turmeric
1 teaspoon ground ginger
1 tablespoon mustard seed

Pour boiling water over the cucumbers and leave for 30 seconds; drain them and place in cold water. Drain again, then slice them crossways into slices 1/2 to 1 cm /1/4 to 1/2 inch thick. Put the sliced onion, peppers and cucumber into a bowl and sprinkle the salt over them. Let stand for two hours, then drain away and discard the liquid.

In a non-corrosive pan, boil the vinegar, sugar and spices for ten minutes, then add the cucumber, onion and peppers. Return to the boil then remove from heat. Pour into sterilized clamp-top jars, leaving a 1-cm/1/2-inch gap at the top and seal. Use the vacuum heat-seal process and store for four weeks for best flavour before eating.

In previous chapters, the culinary properties of vinegar have been examined. We've looked at the many types available, how to make your own vinegar and the uses of vinegar as a key preservative.

If vinegar only served these purposes, its benefits would be well regarded. However, there is so much more available to the consumer from that little bottle hiding away at the back of the cupboard.

In the second section of this book, expect to find the other advantages vinegar has in store – as the most environmentally friendly, non-toxic, deodorizing and disinfecting liquid of all time. This section will cover vinegar's uses:

- as a home remedy
- as a product for home care and DIY
- in activities for children
- in animal care
- in gardening
- in beauty treatments

It seems impossible that one product can offer so many different benefits. It has been known for many years by some as a secret cleaning ingredient.

Tips on how to use it as a window cleaner, a kitchen deodorizer and even a kettle descaler have been passed down from generation to generation.

When mixed with ammonia, borax, dishwashing liquid detergent or bicarbonate of soda (baking soda), vinegar's scouring ability is greatly improved, and all inexpensively and at an extremely low cost to the environment.

Knowledge of vinegar's properties as a home remedy dates back to Hippocrates. Today, vinegar is acknowledged as a gentle yet effective treatment for all manner of ills, including the common cough and cold. It also provides a treatment for arthritis, is an aid to weight loss as a dietary supplement, improves blood circulation and helps with the digestion.

Children will enjoy using vinegar for simple scientific experiments they can perform at home and it can be used to entertain them on rainy days – at economical cost for the parents. The book will show children how to make 'volcanoes', teach them the chemical reaction of vinegar with stone and metal, and how to write with coloured vinegar ink using a quill pen. Above all, they will find out vinegar is a major ingredient in every kid's favourite – toffee.

The home gardener will discover many uses to help with the maintenance and care of the garden, such as killing weeds, removing rust from tools and making azalea plants prosper.

A range of tips for animal care is also included, particularly useful if you want to treat pets or livestock with less toxic products. Most animals will benefit from vinegar – for example, it can keep flies off horses, make a dog's coat shine, stop a chicken from being pecked excessively and deter cats from scratching favourite pieces of furniture.

And at the end of a long hard day looking after everyone else, you can also reward yourself with a few moments for your own care. Vinegar baths, skin treatments, foot massage and even keeping your nail polish looking good for longer are all covered in this book.

Vinegar has been a useful medicine for thousands of years, crossing continents and cultures, assisting doctors and helping ailing populations. While current medicine focuses almost exclusively on complex chemical and drug treatments, vinegar is still being studied for its potential uses in both complementary and orthodox medicine.

As a home remedy, it is reputed to soothe almost anything from joint pain and sore throats to eczema and fatigue and is also beneficial to weight loss. Apple cider vinegar is the favourite therapeutic vinegar and is used in all the remedies featured here. Organic apple cider has further benefits, so whenever possible use it as your remedy base.

It must be stressed that prior to self-diagnosis, it is essential to contact your medical professional to discuss your health problem. The tips featured here are home remedies only and every individual will have a different response to their complaint. In all cases, as with any form of medication or food, should the use of vinegar exacerbate your symptoms, cease treatment immediately and consult your doctor.

Vinegar contains acetic acid, and acid and tooth enamel don't mix well. Be aware that when ingesting vinegar as a remedy, it is best to dilute it with water. Prolonged use of neat vinegar can cause damage to your teeth – so play it safe and water it down.

Ear, Nose & Throat

Swimmer's Ear

The build up of moisture in the ear canal is known as 'swimmer's ear' and when aggravated by the presence of bacteria, it can cause extreme itchiness and pain. Keeping the ear free of water helps dramatically so, every time you come out of the pool, shower or bath, train a hair dryer on each ear for 20 seconds.

If the itchiness is more than you can bear, try a few drops of white vinegar in the ear canal (much like medical ear drops). Ensure the vinegar gets deep into the canal by moving your head slightly. Then, after 30 seconds, allow the fluid to drain out. Aim for two drops for each ear and continue for five days. If this doesn't help, visit your doctor.

Nosebleeds

There are many ways to stop a bleeding nose and vinegar is one of them. Soak sterile cotton strips in vinegar and gently insert into the nostril. Vinegar will then stem the bleeding.

Coughs

If you have a cough that continually keeps you and everyone nearby awake at night, sprinkle a few drops of apple cider vinegar on a cloth and lay it under your head while you sleep.

Sore Throats

There are three ways of treating sore throats – gargling, swallowing and wrapping. If you do all three, the sore throat stands no chance:

● To gargle, mix one teaspoon of apple cider vinegar in a glass of warm water and gargle for ten seconds, three to four times a day.

● To swallow, mix four teaspoons of apple cider vinegar and four tea-spoons of honey in a glass of warm water. Drink every four hours.

● For wrapping, first steep a cloth in a mixture of 200 ml/7 fl oz/1 cup of warm water and two tablespoons of apple cider vinegar. Squeeze it out and place on the throat, keeping it in place by wrapping another scarf or cloth around it. Wear this while sleeping and the vinegar will draw the toxins out of your system.

Colds

No-one likes having a head-cold and once it starts you don't want it to get worse and end up on your chest – particularly if you are an asthma sufferer. One method of arresting a cold's development is to start with a warm bath into which you have poured 500 ml/16 fl oz/2 cups of vinegar. While in the bath, take a flannel (wash-cloth), steep it in the vinegar solution and place it on your chest, keeping it in place for ten minutes. Some people add pepper to the vinegar to draw toxins out of the body. Rinse your chest, stay warm and go to bed. Repeat with a daily bath until the cold starts to leave your body's system.

If winter is approaching, you are likely to be surrounded by people sneezing, coughing and spluttering germs, so prepare this remedy in advance. Soak 100g /3 1/2 oz each of chopped garlic and fresh ginger in 500 ml/16 fl oz/2 cups of apple cider vinegar.

> For blocked noses, the best method is to inhale eucalyptus oil on a handkerchief, but if you add some drops of vinegar as well, you will keep your nose disinfected

Seal in a sterilized bottle until the last month of autumn then, at the end of every meal, drink 10 ml/2 teaspoons of it for two weeks. Be warned, the concoction will have quite a kick!

For blocked noses, the best method is to inhale eucalyptus oil on a handkerchief, but if you add some drops of vinegar as well, you will keep your nose disinfected and help fight off any bacteria in the air.

Bones & Blood

Cholesterol

Fatty foods, smoking, alcohol intake – all these are known to be detrimental to cholesterol levels and if your family is genetically disposed to high cholesterol, you may be at risk of heart disease. Vinegar is known to reduce cholesterol, its acidic nature and rich mineral and trace element content assisting in returning the body to its natural balance.

Combine the fresh juices of fruits that are also known to assist in lowering cholesterol such as apples, cranberries and grapes and add in a tablespoon or two of apple cider vinegar. Drink this every day and your cholesterol count will be reduced.

Arthritis

This is a condition that blights sufferers with painful and stiff joints but the use of apple cider vinegar has consistently been shown to alleviate the pain. Medical stories abound of patients, whose fingers have become deformed by arthritis, finding themselves with pain-free digits thanks to the use of vinegar.

The process is simple. Start with one teaspoon of vinegar a day in a large glass of water. At your own pace, increase this to twice a day and then drink the vinegar with every meal. Over time, increase the vinegar intake to a dessertspoon (two teaspoons) with each glass. Improvement will occur though how great it is depends on the severity of the condition. Do ensure you consult your doctor before commencing the treatment.

Blood Flow

Vinegar is known to greatly assist in thinning the blood because acetic acid restores the alkaline properties of the system. People who suffer from heart conditions should consult their doctor before using vinegar as part of their therapy, as the medication they are using can be seriously affected by vinegar. A teaspoon of vinegar in a glass of warm water taken with every meal can greatly improve your blood's circulation.

People who suffer from heart conditions should consult a doctor before using vinegar as part of their therapy

Feet & Legs

Foot Odour

Smelly feet are no-one's friend and can cause embarrassment. If you suffer from foot odour, soak your feet in a bowl of warm water to which 20 ml/4 teaspoons white vinegar has been added, and do so twice a day for 15 minutes. Continue to do so for ten days and the foot odour will soon cease.

Toenail Fungus

Fungus growth under the toenail can become extremely painful if not treated properly. If possible cut the dead part of the nail off and soak the toe in diluted white vinegar for ten minutes. Repeat this twice daily, once before putting your shoes on and again at the end of the day when you take them off. You can also soak a cotton wool (absorbent cotton) ball in vinegar and rub the toe frequently throughout the day. It may also be worth sterilizing your socks in one part white vinegar to four parts water, before washing them as normal.

Varicose Veins

The process for healing varicose veins depends on the severity of the condition, but apple cider vinegar will certainly assist. There are two methods you can use. The first is massaging the vinegar directly into the affected part of the leg, three times a day. The second is resting the leg by wrapping it in a vinegar-soaked cloth and elevating it for 30 minutes, twice a day. Either method will produce results though the process is slow.

Leg Cramps

Cramp can attack suddenly and without warning. Rub white vinegar into the affected area and the pain will disappear instantly.

Tired Aching Feet

Wearing high-heeled shoes, standing on your feet all day, jogging, going to the gym – these are just some of the things that make our feet think we don't love them. When they start to ache, rub a tablespoon of cider vinegar into them and they will soon feel relaxed and refreshed.

Calluses

Soaking feet in apple cider vinegar, Epsom salts and warm water will assist the healing of calluses on feet. Wash and dry your toes and then apply a cloth soaked in vinegar directly to the callus. Either leave the cloth on for 30 minutes or, to kick-start therapy, tape the cloth in place with sticking plaster and leave it overnight.

Athlete's Foot

For this condition you can use vinegar to clean and disinfect your socks and also apply it to the affected area for relief. Rinse your socks in 500 ml/16 fl oz/2 cups cider vinegar to 2 litres/3 1/2 pints/4 cups water and leave to soak for 30 minutes before washing. For your feet, apply vinegar directly to the area three to four times a day – this should reduce the itching quickly.

> To treat your athlete's feet, apply vinegar directly to the area three to four times a day

Low Energy

Potassium

Potassium is a trace mineral that is a key element for cell and tissue growth. It is also essential in keeping arteries resilient and assisting in blood circulation. Depletion of this mineral can cause numerous symptoms such as:

- Mental and physical fatigue
- Aching bones and muscles
- Sensitivity to cold
- Difficulty in sleeping
- Impatience, memory lapse, forgetfulness
- Itchiness of the skin and scalp
- Tired eyes
- Lower back pain
- Depression
- Nervousness
- Muscle cramps
- Constipation

All or any of these may be an indication of potassium deficiency. The benefit of apple cider vinegar is its high potassium levels, so incorporating this vinegar into your diet can be beneficial. Drink a teaspoon of apple cider vinegar in a glass of water with every meal to increase your potassium levels.

Fatigue

First check your feeling of fatigue with your doctor as excessive tiredness can be the first symptom of many complaints. If it is just the result of too many busy days and nights, mix three teaspoons of apple cider vinegar with 250 ml/8 fl oz/1 cup of honey. Mix two teaspoons of this liquid with hot water just before bedtime and you will feel refreshed the next day.

Insomnia

A mind that won't settle, an inability to find a comfortable place in bed, watching the clock tick through every minute from 4.00 am to breakfast time – all of us have experienced sleeplessness at some stage. For an insomniac, this can happen every night of the week and, apart from leaving a person exhausted, the nervous system can become quite depleted. Vinegar can assist as a nightcap if two teaspoons of honey and two of cider vinegar are dissolved in a glass of warm water. Take a few sips before bedtime and, if you wake in the night, take a few more sips and go back to sleep. Inveterate insomniacs may need to do this a few times but the method will work eventually.

Waste Removal

Urinary Tract

The purpose of the urinary tract is to assist in removal of waste in the body and to do so it requires a certain level of acidity. Infections, bacteria, antibiotics, coffee – all these and many other phenomena can disrupt normal levels of acid, making urination uncomfortable. Vinegar's ability to restore pH levels will assist in restoring the tract to its normal state. A glass of water with a teaspoon of vinegar will help a lot.

Kidneys

Kidney stones form due to a build up of uric acid and calcium. When the stones become dislodged and begin the journey out of the kidneys and through the urinary tract they become excruciatingly painful. Vinegar is well known for its ability to actively dissolve uric acid and calcium and ingesting small amounts of vinegar will reduce the accumulation in the kidneys. Sprinkle vinegar on salads and meat dishes as part of your daily meal or, alternatively, take a teaspoon a day in warm water. This will help to dissolve excess calcium and allow the kidneys to remove the matter easily through the urinary tract.

Cystitis

Bacteria live naturally in parts of the urinary tract but for various reasons the bacteria sometimes travel back into the tract causing discomfort and even bleeding during urination. Taking a teaspoon of apple cider vinegar three times a day will provide relief, but see a doctor if the problem persists for more than five days or if there is blood in the urine.

> When the stones become dislodged and begin the journey out of the kidneys and through the urinary tract they become excruciatingly painful.

Stomach

Stomach Ulcers

The thought of putting any acid on an ulcer would seem ill advised. However it is known that apple cider vinegar assists the stomach in releasing a substance that is beneficial to the gastric system and acts as protection against ulcers. One teaspoon of apple cider vinegar in a glass of water before every meal will do the trick.

Indigestion

Discomfort caused by certain foods does not help your body's process of eliminating waste and absorbing protein, minerals and vitamins. If you suffer from indigestion, in a small ceramic teapot, mix two teaspoons of vinegar and half a teaspoon of green tea and fill with boiling water. Allow the liquid to steep for five minutes then drink as required. Alternatively you can use peppermint tea instead – peppermint greatly assists digestion and is well known for its benefits for upset stomachs.

Weight Loss

There are many diets, pills and potions which help people lose weight but it must be stressed that rapid weight loss in any form can have dire consequences for the body. You will serve your body far better by approaching weight loss gradually, using sensible dieting and regular exercise. Allow your system to adjust to the process. Apple cider vinegar can assist with dieting as it works as a diuretic, draining the body of excess fluid while also reducing the appetite. Take one teaspoon in two cups of warm water before each meal, coupled with regular exercise.

Itches & Scratches

Bites

Apple cider vinegar's ability to draw out toxins is one reason why it is so good for applying to insect bites. As an immediate solution, you can place vinegar directly on the area and rinse it off. Dip a cloth in the vinegar, press it against the bite and the itchiness will cease, sealing some of the broken capillaries at the surface of the skin. If the bite has drawn blood, the vinegar will disinfect the area and prevent further bacteria from entering the wound. If welts occur, make a paste from vinegar and cornflour (cornstarch) and apply it once every two hours until the lumps are reduced.

Hives

These are lumps and bumps on the skin that are the result of allergic reactions and are similar to insect bites. Vinegar will draw out the toxins. Dissolve one tablespoon brown sugar, one teaspoon freshly-grated ginger root and 125 ml/4 fl oz/1/2 cup cider vinegar in 250 ml/8 fl oz/1 cup warm water. Dab the mixture on the affected spot or spots with cotton wool (absorbent cotton) twice a day.

Eczema

Eczema sufferers claim that taking vinegar in their diet has greatly decreased and sometimes even altogether removed their eczema. Vinegar should have the same effect on an eczema rash as it does on other forms of skin irritation, if it is directly placed on the affected area. Pouring a tablespoon or two of cider vinegar in a bath will help a lot also. Some eczema is an internal response to a reaction within the body and in these cases vinegar may not help. If this is the case, medical advice should be sought.

Psoriasis

This very unpleasant and extremely irritating skin condition is mainly treated by keeping the affected part (often the face and head) wet with baths or swimming.

Sometimes hot water can cause further itchiness, so it really depends on what works best for the individual.

To ease an itching scalp, dip a cloth in apple cider vinegar and apply to the scalp or use a final rinse of vinegar in the water after washing your hair.

Haemorrhoids

The presence of haemorrhoids can lead to burning sensations and bleeding, which can be hugely discomforting for the sufferer. You can use undiluted vinegar to assist or, if you find that too strong, dilute it with water. Take a cotton ball dipped in diluted vinegar and gently dab the affected area.

Cold Sores

The cold sore virus is a strain of herpes which remains dormant in the body for long periods of time. Stress, lack of vitamin C, sleeplessness and a cold wind are just some of the factors that can trigger an outbreak around the mouth. Apart from being extremely painful and unsightly, a cold sore can also cause fatigue. It is extremely important at the first sign of a 'tingle' to increase your vitamin C intake. The cold sore will usually run its course, starting with a blister which will then rupture creating the sore itself. At the burst blister stage, apply small dabs of vinegar to the affected area. This will assist in healing the sore much more quickly.

Shingles

Shingles, like cold sores, are caused by a virus and occur under similar conditions, with stress and being physically run down acting as major triggers. Shingles are a far more serious condition than cold sores, however, as they can continue erupting for many, many weeks and are extremely painful. You can apply vinegar direct to the sores but some people find them to be too sensitive – if so, dilute the vinegar with water and apply it three to four times a day.

Jellyfish Stings

In summer, particularly on extremely hot days or after it has rained, these creatures float in large numbers towards the shore with the tide. Bathers can swim along happily unaware of the jellyfish until the skin starts to burn from a sting. To treat the stings immediately, pour vinegar over the affected area to inactivate the stinging cells. Any kind of vinegar will do. If tentacles cling to the skin, avoid touching them with bare skin. Above all do not rub or scratch the skin as this will further inflame it.

Bee Stings

Like jellyfish stings, rinsing the wound with vinegar will greatly reduce the pain or itching. Ensure you first remove the bee's tail (sting) from the puncture wound. Then soak a cloth in neat vinegar and compress it against the sting, holding it there until it has given relief.

Other Complaints

Headaches

If you prefer to avoid taking aspirin, paracetamol or any other chemical treatment to alleviate a headache, vapour inhalation is a valid alternative. In a saucepan, heat together 500 ml/16 fl oz/2 cups apple cider vinegar and 500 ml/16 fl oz/2 cups water; leave the mixture to simmer for five minutes. Pour it into a glass or ceramic bowl, place your head over the bowl and cover your head with a towel. Allow the vapours from the bowl to rise and inhale the fumes from the mixture until the headache starts to subside.

If your headaches are occurring because of blocked sinuses, drink a teaspoon of vinegar in warm water and repeat every four hours until the sinus clears.

Bruises

Just like Jack in the Jack and Jill rhyme, a bruise can be eased with a treatment of vinegar. You can make a cold compress of vinegar and cover the bruise with it or dip the cut side of half an onion into vinegar and rub directly on the affected area to stop the discolouration of bruised skin.

Sunburn

The simplest solution to sunburn is not to put yourself at risk, so stay out of the sun. But if you can't bear to drag yourself away from that beach chair and have forgotten to dowse yourself in suntan lotion and barrier cream, soaking the affected area in a mixture of vinegar and cool water will help alleviate the pain. You can mix 250 ml/8 fl oz/1 cup of vinegar with 125 ml/4 fl oz/1/2 cup natural (plain) yogurt and lightly cover the burn with the mixture every hour until the pain lessens. To remove, rinse the area in cool water and pat the skin dry with a towel.

Do not rub the burn as this will irritate the skin further. Some remedies also add aloe vera, as the juice of this plant is extremely helpful in healing wounds, particularly sunburn.

If you have an aloe vera plant in your home, break off a leaf and add the juice to the vinegar and yoghurt mix.

Mouth Ulcers

Ulcers can be extremely painful, making consumption of food almost unbearable. Gargle with vinegar and this will help in the healing process. Ensure you always rinse with clean water afterwards to protect your teeth.

Gingivitis & Bad Breath

Gargling with vinegar daily will help reduce bleeding from the gums when brushing and will also banish any nasty odours on the breath. Be sure to rinse after gargling as the acetic acid in vinegar can damage the enamel on teeth.

Yeast Infections

There is debate as to whether vinegar is helpful in removing the infection or whether it may actually be a hindrance. Some people advocate treating vaginal thrush by bathing with 500 ml/16 fl oz/2 cups vinegar in the bathwater. This is said to greatly ease the itching.

Other sources indicate, however, that you should completely remove vinegar from your diet as it actually exacerbates the symptoms. As with other vinegar remedies, the best method would be to test the treatment by applying it to a small area first before proceeding with the full course.

Nausea & Vomiting

As a herbal remedy, cloves are known to stop vomiting. Mixing them with warm vinegar and water and then taking as a drink should provide some much needed relief. An alternative is to soak a towel in warmed vinegar and place it on the stomach, replacing it with another towel when the first one goes cold. The vinegar will gradually draw the toxins from your body.

Morning Sickness

Some women suffer dreadful bouts of morning sickness in pregnancy that can even last all day long. Yet it is essential to eat correctly and sufficiently when pregnant. Some form of relief can be found by drinking a teaspoon of honey and a teaspoon of apple cider vinegar in a glass of water. If you still have no relief, consult your doctor.

Boils

While these can be quite painful, the important thing to remember is not to squeeze the boil as this can cause further infection. It is advisable to avoid sugary foods as these can further irritate the boil. To treat a boil with vinegar, dissolve one tablespoon honey and one tablespoon apple cider vinegar and drink the mixture twice a day until the boil subsides. If it worsens, however, place a wet face flannel (wash-cloth) dipped in apple cider vinegar in a microwave oven and heat for 30 seconds on full power. Then pack the flannel on the boil like a heat pack. Continue doing this for 15 minutes, reheating the cloth if it cools down. Repeat three times per day until the boil subsides.

How vinegar became the ideal household cleaner remains a mystery but it has been used around the home for generations. The benefits are amazing. Vinegar is extremely economical and, as we begin to become more conscious of environmental impact, vinegar remains an environmentally friendly product.

It is true that chemicals will offer faster results, but if there are areas in your home that you would like to treat gently, try vinegar and a bit of elbow grease for an equally good result.

The thought of having a whole house smelling of vinegar need not be a worry as the aroma disappears as vinegar dries – to the human nose at least. Animals will still pick up the scent, which is good if you wish to keep them away from certain areas. What follows are handy tips on the wonderful benefits of vinegar, using the most economical type available – white vinegar – chosen particularly for its lack of colour. Always use white vinegar when cleaning unless otherwise specified.

Bathroom

The deodorizing and disinfectant properties of vinegar make it an excellent choice for use in the bathroom. A quick wipe down of all the surfaces in your bathroom with two cups of vinegar added to a bucket of warm water will disinfect the area and prevent mildew from forming. It will also deodorize the entire bathroom so it smells and looks clean and fresh.

Drains can certainly benefit from a little vinegar now and then too. Bicarbonate of soda (baking soda) and vinegar combined work wonders on a blocked drain. Put 100g/2 1/4 oz/2/3 cup bicarbonate of soda and 200 ml / 7 fl oz/1 scant cup vinegar down the drain and leave it for ten minutes. This blend creates a gaseous mixture of carbon dioxide and sodium acetate that will shift anything causing the blockage. Flush clean water through the pipe and your drain should be clear again.

> The deodorizing and disinfectant properties of vinegar make it an excellent choice for use in the bathroom

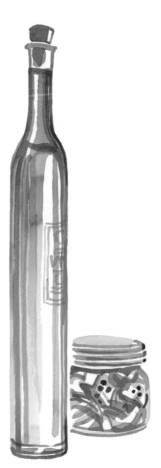

Shower

Showerheads can get clogged with limescale and a general build-up of soap scum and water that can lead to corrosion. To renew your showerhead overnight, either soak a towel in vinegar and leave it wrapped around the shower head or fill a transparent plastic bag with vinegar and tape it across the showerhead, so that the spray area is immersed in the vinegar.

The next day, clean the remaining vinegar from the metal and run water through it – your showerhead will be as clean as new. Alternatively, if you can remove the showerhead itself from the fixture, boil 1 litre /1 3/4 pints/4 cups water with 125 ml/4 fl oz/1/2 cup vinegar and soak the head in the solution for 10 minutes. If the showerhead is plastic, use hot water only, as boiling water may soften it and distort the shape.

Shower curtains can easily become grimy and mouldy with soap scum build-up and are invariably damp. To remove the grime, use full-strength vinegar on a cloth to wipe it down. Alternatively, put the curtain into the washing machine and add 125g/4 oz/1/2 cup detergent, 125g/4 oz/1/2 cup bicarbonate of soda and 125 ml/4 fl oz/1/2 cup vinegar and let the washing machine do the work for you.

Glass and perspex shower doors frequently lose their shine due to build-up of soap scum and limescale. This can easily be fixed with a vinegar mixture of two cups of vinegar in 1 litre /1 3/4 pints/4 cups water. Rub this into the affected area and watch the shine return. Rinse with clean water.

Shower door tracks can also frequently become clogged and can become quite unsightly, breeding mould and germs. You can tackle this with full-strength vinegar if the problem is severe, leaving the door tracks to soak for two hours in the vinegar. A little elbow grease and a good scrub will improve the track greatly. The shower floor is no different to any other area in the shower and can end up stained and grimy. If you have tiles on the floor, the dirt can build up significantly in the grout. This can easily be cleaned by dipping a cloth in vinegar and applying it to the area, rubbing hard and rinsing thoroughly with clean water.

You can also dip an old toothbrush in vinegar for hard-to-get-at areas. After you've finished cleaning, make sure you rinse thoroughly with clean water as vinegar can eat away at tile grout.

Bath

There is nothing nicer than soaking in a long hot bath and it is best to use a clean and shiny bath. To make your bath the best it can be, wash it out with undiluted vinegar, running vinegar around the rim and leaving it for around 30 minutes.

As you would with any bathroom cleaner, use a cloth soaked in hot water and scrub down the area, before giving it a final rinse with clean water. Your shiny new bath is ready for you to relax in.

Taps and other bathroom fittings frequently end up with dirt accumulating around the base, causing them to look grubby. These areas are easily cleaned with a damp cloth soaked in vinegar. Wrap the cloth around the base of the fixtures and leave for 20 minutes then brush away the build-up with a scourer or toothbrush, making sure to give the fitting a final rinse with hot water. Perform a final buff with a soft damp cloth and the shine will return.

Toilet

Several commercial products on the market will make your toilet bowl shine like new. However, if you regularly use vinegar instead, the toilet will become less problematic to clean and you will certainly do the environment a favour by avoiding chemical substances. Place two cups of vinegar in the bowl and leave overnight if possible or at least for a few hours, then flush.

If you have problem grime areas in the bowl, a quick scrub with vinegar will remove staining. The added benefit of using vinegar as a toilet cleaner is its deodorizing effect – all those unpleasant smells will vanish.

Don't forget the toilet seat either – a quick rub down with a cloth soaked in vinegar will destroy bacteria, deodorize the area and further disinfect it.

Water Rings

After a period of time, the surface of water will leave a ring of scum or limescale around any area, as in ring marks on vases. To remove these, a simple method is to soak toilet tissue in vinegar and place it around the mark, then leave it for ten minutes.

A final rinse with clean water should remove the rings, but if the mark is stubborn, rub it with a cloth soaked in hot water and vinegar.

Windows & Mirrors

The most popular, tried-and-tested vinegar treatment is using it to produce clean and shiny windows – without streaks! In fact, vinegar does for glass what fresh air does for a stuffy room.

Use a mixture of equal parts of vinegar and warm water in a clean spray bottle and spray this on the window area. Using a soft cloth, wash the window clean. Then use a chamois leather to dry the window completely. Streaks won't occur and the window will gleam. This method is also excellent for removing fingerprints from glass doors.

Mirrors can be treated in the same way – a quick wipe down with a cloth soaked in a mix of vinegar and hot water, and your mirror will shine anew. If it's the bathroom mirror, you will probably notice watermarks and toothpaste flecks as well.

Dip a cloth in full-strength vinegar and apply to the marks with a little scrubbing. The marks will disappear. Then give the mirror a quick final rub down with vinegar and water.

For weekly mirror maintenance, prepare in a spray bottle:

- 50 ml/2 fl oz/1/4 cup vinegar
- 175 ml/6 fl oz/3/4 cup ammonia (ammonium chloride)
- 16 fl oz/500 ml/2 cups of water

A quick spray on to the mirror once a week followed by a polish with a dry cloth and your mirror will remain dust-free and clean for many days.

Kitchen

As in the bathroom, vinegar works wonders in the kitchen and can be used for everything from cleaning the kettle to cleaning the waste disposal unit. As new materials for cookware and kitchen utensils come on to the market, it is always best to test the vinegar first on a small area just to ensure the material from which it is made will respond to vinegar as required. Then you can clean away to your heart's content.

Smells abound in kitchen areas and sometimes these can become overpowering. A simple solution is to keep a small bowl half-filled with vinegar to deodorize the area. Replace when necessary.

Sink

A waste disposal unit is a useful gadget to have in the kitchen, reducing the amount of waste that has to be thrown out in a waste bin and, in some cases, creating recyclable material that can be used in the garden. But the unit can become extremely smelly. A simple tip is to pour equal quantities of vinegar and bicarbonate of soda into the empty disposal unit, leave for ten minutes then flush through with clean water.

Alternatively, you can freeze vinegar into ice cubes in an ice cube tray and, every now and then, drop a few cubes into the disposal unit. Then switch the unit on with a little cold water running and the smells will disappear. Ensure you flush the unit through finally with clean water, remembering that vinegar can corrode some metals.

The kitchen sink itself accumulates all manner of oil, food scraps and general gunk from washing dishes and making them clean and

sparkly. Subsequently, grime and watermarks start to build up.

To remove grime build-up, pour full-strength vinegar on to the area and leave for a few minutes. A quick scrub will soon shift the dirt but don't forget the all-important final rinse with clean hot water.

To clean the sink's surface, a wipe down with a cloth dipped in neat vinegar will leave it sparkling like new – again, don't forget the all-important final rinse with clean water.

Kettle

Kettles can accumulate lime and mineral deposits. A simple solution is to fill the kettle last thing at night with equal parts of water and vinegar and bring it to the boil – open a window as the vinegar smell will be quite intense. Leave overnight. Then, the next morning, rinse the kettle and fill with clean water again. Then bring to the boil. Rinse the kettle once more and your kettle will now be nice and clean again.

Coffee-Maker

If you live in a hard water area, your coffee-maker is destined to develop mineral deposits. Even with soft water, coffee grinds will build up through several brews, and a brown, murky sludge will accumulate on the bottom and sides. Clean by filling the pot with full-strength vinegar and proceed with a normal brewing cycle. When finished, do the same again, but this time using clean water.

If you use a coffee-pot that you boil on the stove, you can use the same method but use equal parts vinegar and water and ensure to flush it out twice with clean water to remove any taste of vinegar.

Microwave Oven

Now widely used in almost every kitchen, the microwave oven sits quietly on the shelf and dreads the approach of a teenage son with a frozen pizza in hand ready for instant cooking. What lurks on the walls and ceiling of a microwave is anyone's guess – but such stains are also unnecessary as a microwave is so easy to clean.

All you need to do is pour 125 ml/4 fl oz/1/2 cup vinegar and 250 ml/8 fl oz/1 cup water in a glass bowl and place it in the oven. Bring the liquid to the boil in the microwave on full power and continue to boil it on high for another five minutes – or ten minutes if there is a lot of baked-on dirt to be removed. Remove the bowl from the microwave oven and then simply wipe out the inside with a paper cloth.

Chopping Board

There is a modern tendency to use plastic chopping boards instead of those made from wood. This is mainly due to the risk of infection that may arise from germs lurking in the cuts and grooves in the wood. If your preference is for wooden boards, cleaning them is not a difficult task if you use vinegar.

After you have prepared your meal, wash the board with hot water then wipe it with full-strength vinegar. This will destroy any bacteria that may be present.

Stove Top, Hob & Oven

Vinegar is a great degreaser and easily cuts through kitchen food grime. You can either soak a cloth in full-strength vinegar and wipe down the area or mix together, in a plastic spray bottle, 250 ml/8 fl oz/1 cup white vinegar and 125 ml/4 fl oz/1/2 cup bicarbonate of soda. Fill the remainder of the bottle with hot water and spray it on the problem areas.

Leave it to sit for a few minutes, then with a little elbow grease start scrubbing away and soon your stove will be sparkling. Vinegar works exceptionally well on stove tops and hobs, which tend to become greasy every time they are used. Applying spray from the bottle once a week will help keep them clean. Full-strength vinegar poured on a cloth rubbed over a hotplate will remove all manner of spills – burned milk, melted cheese, oil from fry-ups and so forth.

Cleaning the oven can be a tiresome chore, mopping out volumes of burned-on food remains and stubborn grease. Vinegar can assist and, if used regularly, it can also help avoid oven cleaning becoming a dreaded and tiresome task.

In a glass bowl, make a paste of 250 ml/8 fl oz/1 cup vinegar, 50g/2 oz/1/4 cup detergent powder and 125g/4 oz/1/2 cup of bicarbonate of soda. Set your oven to the highest setting and leave it on for five minutes, to heat it up.

Apply the paste to the oven grime and leave it for at least one hour. Scrape off the paste, then remove the rest with a damp cloth.

The first time you do this is likely to be the hardest but regular cleaning with this paste will make it much easier to remove burned-on food and grease from the oven. Once cleaned, wipe the oven down with clean, hot water.

Metal Cleaner

Metal kitchen utensils and cutlery can end up suffering from a dull, grimy appearance thanks to finger marks and general use. To restore your stainless steel, aluminium, copper or brass, vinegar made into a paste with other harmless cleaning substances will bring back their gleam and shine.

It's always best to test a small patch in an inconspicuous spot as metals age and stress in different ways. Once you are certain of the result, apply away.

For stainless steel, dab full-strength vinegar directly on to a soft cloth and apply to the area. Polish with a dry cloth for the best results. Then rinse.

For copper, mix 1 teaspoon salt, 250 ml/8 fl oz/1 cup vinegar and enough flour to make a paste and apply to the copper surface. Let it stand for 10-15 minutes then rinse with clean water. A quick buff with a soft cloth should return the shine to the metal.

For brass, combine 125g/4 oz/1/2 cup of detergent powder, 1 tablespoon salt and 2 tablespoons vinegar to make a paste. Add 500 ml/16 fl oz/2 cups boiling water and gently stir, letting the detergent dissolve. When cool, pour a small amount on to a cloth and rub on the brass until the tarnish is removed. Buff with a dry cloth for the final finish.

If you have cooking pots and pans that you intend to throw away due to the unshiftable gunk at the bottom, give them a second chance by boiling vinegar in them. Then let the pans soak for another half hour and the gunk should be easy to remove.

Refrigerator
An equal mixture of vinegar and water is the best solution for keeping your refrigerator clean. Wipe down regularly and the unit will be disinfected, deodorized and free of food scraps and grease.

Using a vinegar mixture will keep your refrigerator disinfected, deodorized and free of food scraps

Floor Cleaner

Linoleum floors love vinegar – a mixture of equal parts of vinegar and hot water will bring them back to their original state. Be careful not to use this solution on waxed floors, though, as vinegar can cause damage to the surface.

Furniture

Most wooden furniture will benefit from an application of diluted vinegar. You can use it to bring a shine back to wood using 250 ml/8 fl oz/ cup of vinegar in 1 litre/1 3/4 pints/4 cups water. Use a tablespoon of olive oil mixed with two tablespoons of vinegar and rub it into wood surfaces – the oil is good for the wood and the vinegar will bring back the shine.

If you need to repair scratches in wood, a little iodine will assist, mixed in equal parts with vinegar. Work on the principle of more iodine for darker wood and more vinegar for lighter wood – always test an unseen area first before you proceed.

If you enjoy restoring wood and want to bring it back to its former glory, mix 500 ml/16 fl oz/2 cups water with a teaspoon of vinegar and a teaspoon of olive oil. Use this on a scouring pad to remove encrusted dirt and old paint – the oil will work with the wood grain and the vinegar will cut through the dirt.

It's easy to keep leather sofas and chairs in a state of good repair by combining two teaspoons of linseed oil and the same amount of vinegar in a bowl. Rub the mixture on to the leather with a soft cloth and it will come up shiny and clean. This handy solution will also stop the leather from cracking over time.

If you have smokers in the house and want to remove the tobacco smell, place a bowl half-filled with vinegar in the room and the odour will start to disappear. Change the vinegar every couple of days or when necessary.

Car Maintenance

Iced-up windscreens and windows certainly take the fun out of a winter journey. Vinegar is the perfect solution to this particular problem. Try pouring vinegar and warm water across the frozen windshield – the ice will melt and the windscreen should stay clear of frost for a few days. Repeat regularly and the windscreen will stay reasonably clear for long periods.

If you have adorned your car with bumper stickers, removing them can be extremely irritating, particularly as they age, as the glue can cake like hardened plastic. Soak a cloth in full-strength vinegar and apply directly to the sticker. Leave for five minutes and then gently ease it from the windscreen. Further glue residue can also be removed with vinegar.

Carpet in passenger and driver footwells can become really filthy from the driver and passengers stepping from muddy wet roads straight into the car. A mixture of equal parts of water and vinegar sponged on to the stained and dirty area will definitely help.

If you are the owner of an old car, it's worth knowing that a little full-strength vinegar can make the chrome gleam beautifully when applied with a cloth and then buffed to a shine. A mixture of equal parts vinegar and water will even help to revive vinyl upholstery and of course it will make windows, mirrors and headlights shine and sparkle.

Laundry Tips

Vinegar in the laundry room is, in many ways, a godsend, as its versatile properties will clean and remove stains from many types of fabric. Blankets can begin to look tired after a while but can easily be restored with a quick wash in 500 ml/16 fl oz/2 cups vinegar added to the detergent. The vinegar will gently loosen the fabric and subsequently return softness to the material.

White deodorant stains are a common problem. A quick rub with full-strength vinegar for a few minutes before popping the clothes straight into the washing machine should do the trick.

You can always tell how successful a dinner party was by how much wine was spilled on the tablecloth. Even wine can be easy to remove (if done within 24 hours). Sponge full-strength vinegar on to the stain and then rub vinegar into the cloth. Wash the tablecloth as usual in the washing machine and it should be back good as new.

All clothes can benefit from a little vinegar added to the wash, particularly in the last rinse. Build-up of detergent can easily be broken down by 250 ml/8 fl oz/1 cup vinegar – the acid will not harm the clothing and will even soften the fabric.

The risk of the colour running and ruining other fabrics is always a concern, particularly if you have red or black clothing. Dip clothes whose colours may not be fast into white vinegar for a few minutes and then proceed to launder as normal. The vinegar will help keep the colours fast.

Vinegar's ability to break down stains and acid and reduce soapy residue benefits nappies (diapers) and baby clothes. Softness can be restored to the fabric by adding 250 ml/8 fl oz/1 cup to the rinse cycle. This will also assist in deodorizing and further disinfecting the clothing.

Soak white clothes that have turned a lighter shade of grey or yellow in a mixture of one part vinegar to eight parts water. Soak overnight in a non-reactive bowl then launder as normal.

If your tea towels (kitchen towels) have been burned and are slightly scorched, a light rub with a damp vinegared cloth will help remove the burn mark. Use a dry cloth for a final wipe clean – do bear in mind that this technique is good only for light scorch marks.

There is nothing more annoying than discovering you have managed to put your favourite sweater in the washing machine on too high a temperature and it has shrunk. Some hope is available. Soak the garment in its still wet state in a bucket of water containing one part vinegar and two parts water. Leave for 30 minutes then pull the garment back into shape and dry it on a towel, in the shade.

Laundry Tips (cont.)

Vinegar is a great odour-remover, so smelly socks will be a thing of the past. Soak socks in a bucket of hot water containing 500 ml/16 fl oz/2 cups vinegar and leave overnight. Launder as normal and the smell should have gone.

When faced with badly soiled clothes, don't despair, as a soak overnight in warm water to which 250 ml/8 fl oz/1 cup of vinegar has been added will soon have the stains shifted. Vinegar will assist in dissolving all types of stains. Oil-based stains, hair dye, crayons, ink – all can be removed with a little vinegar. Rub into the stained area and leave for a few minutes. If the stain is very hard to shift, use an old toothbrush soaked in vinegar and rub gently into the area. Rinse in warm water and then wash as normal.

Shirts eventually acquire a ring around the collar through general wear and tear but a paste made of three teaspoons bicarbonate of soda and two teaspoons vinegar will remove them. Leave it on the collar for half an hour then put the shirts in the washing machine. When the shirts are washed, the stain around the collar should have gone. It might also be worth rubbing a little vinegar into the armpit area as this is likely to need odour removal.

Linen is beautiful to wear but extremely tiresome to iron. Before you start, spray a mixture of three parts water to one part vinegar on the cloth and leave for ten minutes. The vinegar odour will disappear as the linen dries and the fabric will be much easier to iron.

Steam-irons need their own special steam-clean, particularly as the water in steam-irons can leave calcium and lime deposits. Partially fill the reservoir with vinegar and steam the vinegar out. Rinse with water and then fill the reservoir with water again, letting all out again as steam. Then use as normal.

Sewing

When hems are being let down or when a fabric has been tacked before sewing, holes may be left where the cotton once ran through the material.

If you dampen the holes with equal parts of vinegar and water then iron the fabric, the holes will disappear.

If you dampen hem holes with equal parts of vinegar and water then iron the fabric, the holes will disappear

Vinegar is a natural disinfectant and ideal for cleaning parts of the house used by babies and children

Cleaning for Kids

Vinegar is a natural deodorizer and disinfectant and it is particularly suitable for cleaning parts of the house used by babies, toddlers and children. Highchairs, babies' bottles, children's toys – all will benefit from a spray from a bottle containing one part vinegar and one part water wiped down with a soft cloth.

● Babies' bottles should be soaked for two hours in vinegar then rinsed thoroughly in hot water. Sterilize the bottles as normal before filling the bottle with milk or water.

● Highchairs seem to have food hidden in every nook and cranny. Use a soft toothbrush dipped in vinegar to clean, then wipe down thoroughly after cleaning.

● Clean and disinfect plastic baby toys with a cup of vinegar and a squirt of dishwasher liquid in hot water. Give them a final rinse in clean hot water and leave to dry.

Outdoor children's toys, whether the tricycle or the swing set, will all become far dirtier because they live outside. A paste of two teaspoons bicarbonate of soda and three teaspoons vinegar can be used to remove dirt and bring such items right back to life. After scrubbing the toys, always rinse them in hot water, particularly any metal parts.

Chewing gum is every parent's worst nightmare when it comes to cleaning, particularly when it is discovered on the carpet or the sofa. Remove as much gum as possible and then soak the residue in full-strength vinegar and leave for 15 minutes. Once done, then remove.

Glue-Remover

Vinegar is the ideal solvent for removing adhesives:

On glass, apply vinegar to a cloth and soak the area of the adhesive for ten minutes. The glue should come off easily when gently scraped.

To remove old stickers, paint vinegar on the area and leave for half an hour. The sticker should start to come away, but if it has been there for many years you may need to ease it off gradually.

For removing old labels, rub vinegar over the area and leave for a few minutes before peeling the label off.

Scissors also end up with bits of sticky mess between the blades which can become frustrating when trying to cut straight lines. Rub a cloth dipped in full-strength vinegar on to the blades until the glue and grime is removed.

Carpet

The first thing to do before proceeding with vinegar as a carpet cleaner is to test it on a part of the carpet that is hidden from view. Carpets these days are made from many different dyes and mixtures of yarns, and vinegar could affect the colour of the carpet.

Mix one teaspoon vinegar and two teaspoons dishwashing liquid. Pour this into a spray bottle, then fill the rest of the bottle with warm water. Place a few drops of the spray on to the test area and, if there is no damage, spray on to the stain. Rub gently across the stain area then blot the liquid with a paper towel. Repeat until the stain has gone and finally blot with a clean cloth dampened in hot water.

If you are treating a 'pet accident', sprinkle white vinegar over the area and leave for a few minutes. Blot from the centre of the stain outwards and use a sponge to clean the area, finally drying with a damp cloth. You may need to do this several times, depending on the severity of the stain, but thanks to the smell of vinegar, the pet is unlikely to return to create the same problem again.

Venetian Blind

Cleaning these can be a simple task with a little vinegar and water on an old cotton sock. Put your hand inside the sock and dip it in the liquid. Then wipe each of the slats. The dust will return of course, but continual use should see it diminish.

Wallpaper Solvent

Removing wallpaper is never a fun job so try a solution of white vinegar to assist you. Dilute 250 ml/8 fl oz/1 cup white vinegar in 2-3 litres/ 3 1/2-5 1/4 pints/8-12 cups of hot water, as hot as you can bear. Apply with a sponge and, as soon as the wallpaper begins to peel away, apply the liquid behind the paper, against the adhesive, to work it away from the wall.

If you keep the area damp, the warm water and the vinegar will help you further. When the water starts to cool, make a new solution and then continue.

Watermarks on Wood

Whether it's your coffee cup or a cold wine glass, the ring that can be left behind on wood is unsightly. Rings can easily be removed with a mixture of equal parts of vinegar and olive oil, rubbing the solution into the grain of the wood and then giving the wood a final polish with a soft cloth.

Shoes

After a good polish, buff leather shoes with a few drops of vinegar on a soft cloth and the leather will shine brilliantly. When cleaning suede, you should always tackle small areas, working slowly. Suede shoes tend to accumulate small shiny spots from wear and sometimes they get stained with water. Put a drop of vinegar on to the area, let it dry and then buff with a suede brush. Vinegar works exceptionally well on patent leather shoes too – a quick rub with a vinegar-soaked cloth and they will gleam.

Leather shoes often acquire white marks from being worn in the rain. A rub down with a cloth soaked in vinegar will remove the stains but make sure you polish the shoes with a dry cloth afterwards.

Flowers

Coming home to a lovely bunch of fresh-cut flowers is a joy. The blooms will stay fresh for you if you add a teaspoon of sugar and two tablespoons of vinegar to the vase's water.

Vinegar can assist with creating activities for you to do with your kids, while also providing safe medicinal treatments and helping in the care of household pets and animals.

Kids' Stuff

Easter Eggs

With the wealth of chocolate available at Easter, there is nothing more special than receiving an individually home-made Easter egg. Presenting a gift of brightly coloured eggs is such a treat and they are something your children will love to create. Combine one teaspoon of white vinegar with 125 ml/4 fl oz/1/2 cup boiled water and add one teaspoon of food colouring.

Gently dip the egg into the mixture until you achieve your intended colour. It's a similar process to watercolour painting – the more you dip, the more intense the colour will be. You can mix the colours, with blue on one end and yellow on the other, and you can even paint the mixture on to the egg. The vinegar will ensure the dyes stay bright and will keep the colour consistent across the shell.

No-Shell Eggs

This is something of a magic trick and requires supervision of younger children. Place an egg at room temperature in a jar and add enough white vinegar to cover the egg. Cover the jar and refrigerate it for 24 hours. The vinegar will start to dissolve the eggshell during this time. Carefully remove the jar from the refrigerator and pour away the vinegar.

Repeat the process again, covering the egg with fresh vinegar and leaving it for a further 24 hours in the refrigerator. What you should eventually be left with is an egg without a shell, but if the membrane around the egg breaks, throw it away mmediately as it will start to smell bad.

Vinegar Quill Pens

Find a large feather, such as a goose feather, sometimes available at craft stores, and cut the tip of the quill at an angle, placing a small slit in the tip.

Place 125g/4 oz/1/2 cup of juicy berries, such as blueberries, raspberries, loganberries or blackberries, in a fine-meshed sieve and, using a metal spoon, push them against the sieve to release the juices. Discard the berry pulp and keep the juice. To the juice, add 1/2 teaspoon salt and 3/4 teaspoon of white vinegar. Then dilute with water until the ink has the consistency you prefer.

When you are satisfied, dip the quill into the ink and create beautiful hand written material using your own ink. This recipe will make a small amount of ink that can be stored in a jar or bottle with a tight-fitting cap.

When you are satisfied, dip the quill into the ink and create beautiful hand-written material using your own ink

Vinegar Volcano

This is great fun, particularly for any budding young scientist, but, be warned, it should be done outdoors, away from any precious objects, as once the children get the hang of it you could be dealing with a miniature Pompeii.

The first step in producing your volcano cone is to make a dough from 750g/1 lb 10 oz/6 cups plain (all-purpose) flour, 500g/18 oz/2 cups coarse (kosher) salt, 4 tablespoons vegetable oil and 500 ml/18 fl oz/2 cups of water. To create your desired colour add 3-4 drops of food colouring to the mixture. Mix together until the coloured dough is firm but still pliable, like a biscuit (cookie) dough.

You can add more water to make it smoother if need be. Decide how big you want your volcano to be, using a bottle as the interior structure. Place the bottle on a level, firm surface and mould your volcano cone dough around the bottle, increasing the steepness of the angle as required. The narrowest end of the cone should stop 2 mm/1/6 inch from the rim of the bottle. Ensure no dough drops inside the bottle or covers the opening. Allow the dough time to dry – approximately two to three hours, depending on how thick you have made it.

When dry, prepare to cause the eruption. Using a funnel, pour warm water and a couple of drops of red food colouring into the bottle, filling it almost to the brim, but stopping within 7.5 cm/3 inches of the opening. This will be a tricky thing to judge when the bottleneck is covered with dough, but if you use a funnel you can

determine when to stop pouring in water when it reaches the bottom edge of the wide part of the funnel.

Alternatively, cut a 10-cm/4-in strip of paper and clearly mark the 7.5-cm/3-inch point on it. Place the paper so it sits vertically in the bottleneck. As you start to fill the bottle, pull the paper out and check the end – if it is wet, you will have an idea of how much more water you need to add until you reach the mark.

Then, once your bottle is filled, add six drops of washing-up liquid (dishwasher liquid) to the bottle contents and two tablespoons bicarbonate of soda (baking soda). Remove the funnel, then slowly pour two tablespoons of white vinegar into the bottleneck and stand well back as your volcano erupts!

Vinegar Toffee

One of the best things about being a kid is making your own sweets (candies), and toffee (taffy) is about as sweet a sweet as can be found. Line a baking tray (cookie sheet) with miniature cake-baking paper cases. Spray them with baking spray if you don't want the toffee to stick to them. Have a bowl of cold water next to you. In a non-reactive pan, mix together 660g/1 lb 7 oz/2 3/4 cups granulated sugar, 250 ml /8 fl oz/1 cup water and 60 ml /2 1/4 fl oz/5 tablespoons malt vinegar.

Stir the mixture over a low heat until the sugar has dissolved. Bring the syrup to the boil. When it is boiling, dip a teaspoon into it and drop a little into the bowl of cold water – it should set instantly.

When it has reached that point, remove the pan from the heat and spoon the mixture into the paper cases. Then sprinkle each toffee with hundreds-and-thousands (colored sprinkles). Place the tray in the refrigerator to let the toffee harden.

Doughnuts

Doughnuts are great to make with kids on a rainy day but they tend to go soggy unless you make the dough with vinegar. Before you add the dough to the frying fat or oil, beat a teaspoon of white vinegar into it and stir until the dough is smooth. The vinegar will stop the doughnuts from becoming too greasy and they will keep longer when stored.

Kid's Clay

This is a great home craft idea for kids, extremely economical and, with supervision, something kids can make by themselves. Mix 250g/ 8 oz/2 cups plain (all-purpose) white flour, 250g/8 oz/1 cup coarse (kosher) salt, one teaspoon vinegar and 125 ml/4 fl oz/1/2 cup water. Knead the dough until soft and then divide into smaller portions. Colour each portion with food colouring to make different coloured clays. Store in the refrigerator, wrapped in plastic, until you want to use it, then bring it to room temperature and use for modelling.

Balloons Galore!

This tip is useful for all parents preparing for their child's next birthday party. In a clean, empty bottle, mix two table-spoons water and one teaspoon bicarbonate of soda (baking soda). Stretch your balloon, then quickly add four tablespoons of white vinegar to the mixture in the bottle. Fit the balloon opening over the neck of the bottle and watch the balloon inflate. Adding the vinegar to the water and bicarbonate of soda creates carbon dioxide, which is released in the bottle in a gaseous reaction. Kids will think it's a trick and, as parents, your cool status will inflate (and you'll have saved your lungs).

Stinky Lunchboxes

Children often leave used lunchboxes in their school bags over the weekend and they are then discovered on Sunday night, smelling nasty due to their content of half-eaten apples and mouldy bread. Here's a tip to remove the smell: empty the box, dampen a fresh piece of bread with white vinegar and leave it overnight in the lunchbox. The next day, discard the bread, rinse out the box and it will smell fresh again – ready for the same thing to occur the following weekend!

Rock Excavators

Take your child on an imaginary journey in ancient times, travelling along unknown paths, seeking new lands, only to find the road is blocked with impassable boulders. And all they have in their saddle-bag is a bottle of white vinegar. They may feel defeated but they have the best excavating tool available.

To show them what they could do, find a small jar and place a piece of stone in it made of limestone, calcite or chalk. Pour the vinegar over the stone and place it in the sun. The vinegar, assisted by the sun's heat, will start to dissolve the calcium carbonate and other minerals in the stone, eventually breaking it apart.

> Take your child on an imaginary journey in ancient times, travelling along unknown paths, seeking out new lands

Sailing Bottles

This project will work best with a pond as your harbour but, if you can't retrieve the bottles, it's better to use a toddler's wading pool or the bathtub. Take a length of toilet paper and put three tablespoons of bicarbonate of soda (baking soda) in it.

Wrap it up tightly, twisting or folding the ends so the contents cannot escape. Place the paper package in a lightweight bottle and add 50 ml/2 fl oz/1/4 cup of vinegar, then quickly secure the bottle with a cap, but do not turn it too tightly. Put the bottle in the water and watch it move.

The reaction between the vinegar and the bicarbonate of soda creates a fizzy, volatile mixture of carbonic acid, which propels the bottle through the water. Add a few bottles, each containing drops of different food colourings in the vinegar and you can have your very own regatta.

Vinegar Designs

This is another rainy day activity, a great craft for children wanting to make their own posters, cards or paintings. You can use any type of white paper as the base, depending on what you want the final product to look like.

Cards will need to be made of thick, strong paper, whereas posters can be made with photocopier paper. You need a range of coloured tissue paper – red, green, pink, blue, etc. – for cutting into shapes, such as hearts for red tissue, stars for pink tissue, squares for blue tissue – whatever your young artist wants to create.

Pour white vinegar into a bowl and, with a paint brush, paint vinegar over the whole of the white paper. Place your shapes on the paper, pressing down so the entire shape sticks to the surface, then leave the paper to dry. The vinegar on the white paper will dry and the tissue paper shapes will fall off – but the imprint from the ink will remain.

Vinegar Conkers

Most kids these days hardly even know what the game of conkers is, unless there's an electronic version! But you can take them back to the games of old and show them how to make a conker that no-one can defeat – by secretly soaking the conker in vinegar, baking it a little and ending up with a completely toughened outer shell.

To do this properly, get your child to place their best conker into 125 ml/4 fl oz/1/2 cup white vinegar for two minutes, then take it out and, with adult supervision, place it in the oven at 250°C (475°F) for 1 1/2 minutes. Remove the conker and let it cool. Pierce a hole in the conker and thread a 12-inch/30-cm piece of string through it, then tie the string in a knot. Your child now has a conker to challenge any other.

Magic Beans

Take a clear vase and fill it with water, add 50 ml/2 fl oz/1/4 cup white vinegar and three teaspoons of bicarbonate of soda (baking soda). Drop dried beans into the vase. These should rise to the top, then drop, then rise again. A few spell castings and abracadabras should qualify you as the most magical parent on the block!

Money Cleaners

An interesting experiment is placing copper coins halfway into a solution of vinegar and watching as the immersed half of the coins come out looking shiny and new. Make sure the solution of vinegar is in a glass, not in a vessel made of metal. When the coin is rinsed, it will have a shiny half but, if the coin remains unrinsed, this will start to turn a blue-green colour as the vinegar reaction continues.

Animals, Animals, Animals

Fleas

A pet with fleas is not good for your house or the people who live in it but, most of all, for the poor pet itself. Pets with allergies to fleas have the worst time of all and frequently owners have to resort to chemical products to help poor Rover or Whiskers.

If you are looking for something a little more environmentally friendly for their treatment or even if you want to use something in conjunction with prescribed care, vinegar can assist. Add a teaspoon of white vinegar to 500 ml/16 fl oz/4 cups of their drinking water on a daily basis.

Soon you will find the fleas are not fond of the taste of the animal's skin and they will soon start to disappear, which will come as a great relief to your beloved pet – and therefore you as well.

Toilet Training

Every pet that has the luxury of living in the owner's home must go through this process. Sadly, it doesn't always go to plan and the last thing you want is the evidence all over your carpet.

There is hope though. First find a piece of the carpet that is unobtrusive, either under the stairs or in the closet. With a few drops of white vinegar, test the area to ensure the strength of vinegar will not damage the colour of the carpet.

Once happy with the result, sprinkle white vinegar across the fresh 'accident' and let it sit for a few minutes. Blotting from the centre of the stain outwards, use a sponge to clean the area and when satisfied with the result, pat the area with a dry cloth.

Depending on the severity of the stain, you may need to do this several times. The vinegar will help remove both the stain and the bad smell.

Smelly Cats

Even if a cat is toilet-trained, its litter box can still create wafts of unpleasantness. However, you can rinse the litter box with detergent, then mix 125 ml/4 fl oz/1/2 cup of white vinegar with 1 litre/1 3/4 pints/4 cups of water, place it in the litter box and allow it to stand for ten minutes. Rinse the box again with fresh water as traces of the vinegar scent could deter the cat from using the box. Once clean and sparkling, the litter box will smell far better and be disinfected and deodorized as well.

Smelly Dog

Dogs have a wonderful habit of finding the most putrid smells in strange places then rolling around until their coats smell the same. Proudly they will return home. The thought of a full bath can fill an owner with dread. Instead you can use a vinegar bath. Add 125 ml/4 fl oz/ 1/2 cup lavender vinegar in 1 litre/1 3/4 pints/4 cups water, dip your sponge in it, then use it to give your dog a

quick rub down. The vinegar will remove the dreadful smell, disinfect your animal and leave your dog smelling like a fresh posy.

Ear of the Dog

Dogs can get dreadful infections in their ears, causing them great pain and making them scratch, usually resulting in a lampshade hat for the canine. There are many chemical products available to help, but a cheaper and more environmentally friendly method is to use vinegar.

Dip a soft, moistened cloth in a small amount of vinegar to wipe the inside of the animal's ear. The disinfectant in the vinegar will keep the ears clean and dry and also assist in controlling bacteria within the ear.

Naughty Cats & Dogs

Most often, the word 'no' really doesn't make sense to the cat who loves to scratch your favourite chair or the dog that chews up your best shoes. If you mix 125 ml/4 fl oz/1/2 a cup of vinegar and one cup of water in a spray bottle, when the offending animal behaves in the usual manner, a quick spurt will soon deter it. The spray is harmless to the animal. If the behaviour still occurs when you are out of the house, sprinkle a little vinegar on the item and the animals will stay away.

Birds & Parrots

Caged birds can sometimes suffer illnesses caused by the environment in which they are kept. Apart from the proprietary products on the market, a simple means of maintaining aviary health is regular cleaning with vinegar and water. Cages made with some types of wires containing zinc can be harmful to birds, particularly parrots, but a regular wipe of the cage

with vinegar will reduce the chance of poisoning. Cleaning perches, floors, food- and water-containers with vinegar and water will also help, particularly in disinfecting the build-up of hardened droppings that can prove to be extremely difficult to remove.

A Horse's Coat

Products on the market that claim to make your horse's coat gleam can be quite expensive. A much cheaper solution is to use vinegar. Mix 125 ml/4 fl oz/1/2 cup of vinegar with 1 litre/1 3/4 pints/4 cups water, then put the mixture in a spray bottle and spray it over the horse. The end result? Your horse's coat will now shine like a glittering diamond.

No Flies

The swarms of flies around horses can make your horse very unhappy, particularly if the flies bite it. If you add 50 ml/2 fl oz/1/4 cup of vinegar to the horse's feed, you will soon see a dramatic reduction in the flies, and the bites will also disappear. Apple cider vinegar is the best option as the horse will like the taste as well.

In the Farmyard

Cows benefit greatly from vinegar. Adding small amounts to their daily feed will enable them to produce more milk. When adding a new cow to the herd, a quick spray of vinegar and water will ensure the animal is accepted easily into the group. And, if you want to produce better beef at market, add two tea-spoons of vinegar to their water daily to tenderize the meat. The term 'pecking order' comes from chickens pecking each other, to determine who is top chicken. Sometimes, however, the chickens can damage each other by this behaviour. To avoid this, pour a little vinegar into their water and they will soon stop. There is a further benefit – adding vinegar to their water will assist their growth.

Vinegar is widely used in the livestock industry for its disinfectant properties. Peracetic acid – a mixture of hydrogen peroxide and vinegar – is a simple and inexpensive disinfectant, and extremely useful method of killing bacteria and viruses.

White Line Disease

This is a fungus that can cause great problems in horse's hooves, making them sore and painful. If you suspect the presence of White Line Disease, make sure that you first check with your vet.

Create a solution of 125 ml/4 fl oz/1/2 cup white vinegar, 250 ml/8 fl oz/1 cup copper sulphate and 2 litres/3 1/2 pints/8 cups water. Then place the infected hoof in this to soak for 15 minutes each day and repeat for the next 5-7 days – it should clear the fungus away.

For many centuries, the Japanese have understood the benefits of vinegar as a beauty aid and, as Western consumers continue to seek natural and skin-friendly therapies, vinegar sits in the cupboard as the quiet achiever. The main thing to remember is not to allow vinegar near the eyes as the acid can be harmful. Apple cider vinegar has been used for all the beauty recipes featured within these pages.

In gardening, the benefits of vinegar have long been acknowledged. It is an effective and environment-ally friendly alternative to chemicals, offering amazing results at a fraction of the price of proprietary products.

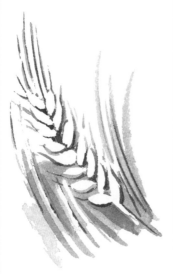

Skin

Skin is deeply affected by diet, the environment and the stresses of daily life, so it deserves the very best care. Vitamin C is an extremely important component for skin and, with the help of vinegar, it is easily digested by the body, so drink a teaspoon of apple cider vinegar in a glass of water each day. Vinegar also helps to restore the natural pH balance of the skin.

Vinegar Peel

The function of a cosmetic peel is to release the epidermis of the skin, removing a layer to expose the layer underneath. The theory is that the new skin promotes a fresher, younger-looking appearance but the process can be quite expensive. It also needs to be a gentle treatment: if performed too harshly, faces can look as if they are severely sunburned. A simpler and less expensive variation, which can be used as a home remedy, is the vinegar peel. Wash your face and then apply vinegar directly on the skin; leave for five minutes. Rinse the vinegar off and your skin will feel and look much fresher. The skin will also be sensitive to sunlight however, so stay out of direct sunlight for an hour afterwards.

Ageing Gracefully

As we grow older, our skin changes and the clearest indicator of this is age spots. There are many creams and potions available that claim to remove them, but the tried-and-tested natural method is to use apple cider vinegar. Combine it with your normal moisturiser, directly applying the vinegar on to the spots or even mixing it with onion juice. The blemishes should eventually start to lighten. If you fear you willl smell of vinegar and onions, mix a quantity of your regular moisturizing lotion with half as much vinegar. Use regularly and the spots will continue to lighten over time.

Blackheads

Blackheads are annoying and unsightly, the result of having a greasy skin or teenage acne. As a means of removing and avoiding them further, the astringent property of strawberries when mixed with vinegar provides a natural deep cleanser. Combine 1/3 cup vinegar with five chopped strawberries and leave at room temperature for a few hours. Strain the liquid through a sieve and discard the strawberry pulp. Dab the liquid on to the area affected by blackheads before bedtime. The next morning rinse off and repeat until the blackheads clear.

Acne

Every teenager's dread, acne can cause embarrassment and loss of self-esteem. A huge array of expensive cosmetics are available which claim to combat acne, including masks, cleansers, toners and scrubs, and it is often a matter of finding which one works best for your skin. A useful remedy that is economical and easy to make is a mixture of one teaspoon vinegar to ten teaspoons water. Pour it into a small, easily portable bottle with a tight-fitting cap and, throughout the day, dab it on to spots and pimples.

The vinegar mixture will help the skin back to its normal pH balance. Another home remedy is to make a paste consisting of two teaspoons apple cider vinegar, one teaspoon of honey and one teaspoon of flour. Leave this on overnight and rinse off in the morning.

Always test it first on one blemish; if it is effective, the blemish should heal faster.

Oily Skin, Flaking Skin

Clean skin protects the body but also absorbs pollution in the environment, the pores showing the evidence of oil and dirt build-up. Whether your skin is oily or dry, apple cider vinegar is rich in acids that help to dissolve fat and reduce flaking while promoting a softer, smoother complexion. A mixture of equal parts apple cider vinegar and water applied to the face, allowed to dry, then finally rinsed with water will allow your skin to breath easily and look fresher.

Magic Home Remedy Night Cream

The sheer cost of commercially produced skin treatments is enough to make you believe that they work. Yet you can create your own natural (and economical) treatments that will work just as well. Mix 125 ml/4 fl oz/1/2 cup olive oil with three teaspoons apple cider vinegar, diluted with enough water to make a cream. Apply small amounts to your face before bedtime and rinse off the next day with water. Your skin will feel moisturized and cleansed – and you'll have more spending money left as well.

Even men can get in on the apple cider vinegar treatment. As an aftershave, small amounts of vinegar will keep shaved skin disinfected and keep the skin looking good.

Hair

The acetic acid in vinegar works similarly to lemon juice when lightening strands of hair. So if you want the summery look but without the expense of proprietary streaks, use a cotton ball soaked in vinegar and ease it through the strands of hair you want to bleach. Spend some time in the sun and watch how the colour develops. You can get creative and make variations with lemon juice and vinegar but first take a strand and test it to see what colours will appear. Vinegar will eventually lighten hair, but, if you are a brunette, it will first turn it red.

Frizz Control

Curly hair and frizzy hair can both get out of control but vinegar has a smoothing effect. When you have washed your hair, rinse it with a mixture of 250 ml/8 fl oz/1 cup vinegar and 250 ml/8 fl oz/1 cup water. Leave this on the hair for two minutes then rinse. You will find the frizz factor lessens and continued use will eventually smooth the hair follicles.

Dandruff

There are many variations of vinegar's magical cure for dandruff. Some suggest applying undiluted vinegar directly to the scalp, while others say it should be combined with water and left on the hair for several hours. Some recipes advocate mixing it with aspirin to form a paste. However it is used, the essence remains the same – vinegar will restore the pH content of hair over time, reducing soap build-up and making the scalp more supple.

Rinses & Conditioners

All shampoo and conditioning products create a build-up within the hair over time. Adding hairspray, mousse, gel or colourant also deadens the hair over a significant period. Instead of using your own conditioner, try a vinegar conditioner as a replacement. This will reduce the chemical accumulation and restore the hair to its natural shine. Be sure not to let the vinegar get into your eyes as the acetic acid will burn them.

Here are a few different recipes:

Oil & Vinegar Rinse

Beat two whole, raw eggs with one tablespoon olive oil and 3/4 teaspoon vinegar and apply to your hair, leaving the mixture on for half an hour.
Rinse out with water.
Your hair will come up shiny and smooth.

Vinegar Hair Conditioner

Slightly bruise three sprigs of rosemary and one tablespoon of sage, then place them in a non-reactive pan adding 125 ml/4 fl oz/1/2 cup apple cider vinegar and 125 ml/4 fl oz/1/2 cup water. Let the mixture simmer for ten minutes. Cool to room temperature, allowing the mixture to steep, then strain into a bottle. After shampooing, use the mixture as a conditioner, leaving it on the hair for two minutes before rinsing. The rosemary will add body to the hair, sage will reduce the oiliness and the vinegar will create a lustrous shine.

Baths

Helen of Troy was known to believe in vinegar baths as a means of softening and cleansing the skin. There are many variations, starting with the basic method of adding 1 litre/1 3/4 pints/4 cups apple cider vinegar to the water. Herbs, rose petals, camomile and even salt can be added to enhance the luxury of the bath, the vinegar adding the restorative power of returning the pH balance to the skin. Here are a few suggestions:

Mint Vinegar Bath

While running the bath, sprinkle a handful of bruised mint leaves and 250 ml/8 fl oz/1 cup apple cider vinegar in the hot water. Then leave the bath for a few minutes before climbing in. The aroma of the mint will refresh and the vinegar will restore an aching body.

Rose Petal & Rosemary Vinegar Bath

As for the Mint Vinegar Bath, bruise a few twigs of rosemary under the hot water, add 250 ml/8 fl oz/1 cup vinegar and sprinkle fresh rose petals over the water. Leave the bath water for one minute before entering. The rosemary will stimulate the skin as the vinegar softens it and the rose petals will make you smell wonderful.

For every bath, use 250 ml/8 fl oz/1 cup apple cider vinegar and add these combinations:

- Six stems lavender flowers
- One tablespoon almond oil
- As many camomile flowers as desired
- 50g/2 oz/1/4 cup dried thyme & sage
- 125g/4 oz/1/2 cup chopped lemongrass
- Peel of one orange or one lemon

Vinegar Massage

Tired, aching bodies can easily be renewed with this recipe. You can use any type of scented oil – peppermint to refresh, lavender to relax, rose to soothe – just mix one teaspoon oil with 500 ml/16 fl oz/2 cups apple cider vinegar and 500 ml/16 fl oz/2 cups water. Find a friend to give you a massage or massage your own feet for relief.

Nails & Hands

Keep your nail polish looking fresh a little longer by first preparing your nails with vinegar. Dip your nails in two teaspoons vinegar and 125 ml/4 fl oz/1/2 cup warm water for one minute. This will clean the nail and keep the polish on longer.

Vinegar does such wondrous things for the rest of your body, don't forget to let your hands in on the secret also. To stop them drying out and chapping, rub a little vinegar into them and they will instantly soften. If you are going to work in the garden in winter, a little vinegar on the hands will keep your fingers supple while you work.

Gardening

It is possible to use standard white distilled vinegar for gardening purposes and, in some cases, while the process may take longer, the benefits of using 5% acetic acid may serve the soil better. Vinegar is acidic and needs to be used sparingly and directly to the problem areas, particularly if you are using gardening vinegar, the acetic acid level of which is 20%.

This vinegar is sold at garden centres and hardware stores and is strictly for outdoor use only. It must never be used in the same way as vinegars for cooking or home remedy purposes since its high acidity is corrosive. Read the instructions before use, protecting clothing and skin when applying. Ensure that any other container in which you store it is non-reactive as vinegar corrodes metal. Domestic white vinegar can be used for the purposes listed here – while the results may be slower, it remains effective.

Weeds

Weeds that grow in crevices and cracks in the concrete between footpath and driveway can be tackled with a dose of white vinegar. If the weather is hot, vinegar works even better. Pour it directly on to the roots of the weed, continuing every three to four days until it dies. For older weeds, you may need to do this on a daily basis as they will be tougher to remove, but if you can get to the weed when it first shoots through, you will have a better success rate. The same applies to grass growing in unwanted areas; be careful not to spray it on grass you want to keep.

Pests

Slugs will face certain demise with vinegar. Mix equal parts of vinegar and water in a spray bottle, give them a few squirts and they will go away to die. Alternatively, pour equal quantities of beer and vinegar into an old saucer. The slugs will be attracted by the beer – and the vinegar will kill them.

Rabbits love vegetables and, while your garden seems to be their favourite supply, there is a simple and easy solution to deter them. Soak cotton balls in white vinegar and place them in small containers around the vegetable patch. The rabbits will be deterred by the vinegar smell and leave your vegetables to prosper in peace.

Plant Pots

Plastic plant pots and saucers that are regularly soaked in water will build up white mineral stains and crusts on their rims. These can be easily cleaned away by submerging them in white vinegar and leaving them to soak for over an hour. The pots should clean up as good as new. Mould and algae can also grow on terracotta pots, but soaking them in equal parts of vinegar and bleach in a bucket of water will assist in shifting the stain. You may still need to scrub with steel wool but the residue will shift far more easily than if you just use detergent.

Avoid spraying vinegar on weeds or unwanted grass on windy days. The vinegar spray can easily be deflected and start its acidic reaction on plants you love

Ants

Ants will gather from outside the house and wander their way inside, into cupboards and into your food. If you follow the ant trail and sprinkle a line of white vinegar along it, the ants will soon avoid the path. Ants have a strong sense of smell and will be attracted to their favourite foods inside your pantry, such as honey, even from miles away.

Mosquitoes & Midges

If you live somewhere where these are rife in the summertime, it's a matter of putting endless chemical substances on your body as a deterrent. You may be enjoying a barbecue when you discover you have run out of mosquito repellant. In your cupboard, however, you have a cheaper and more environmentally-friendly solution in the shape of vinegar. Rubbing a little apple cider vinegar on the exposed skin will deter the bloodsuckers and they will leave you and your guests in peace.

Moths

On a hot summer evening, there is nothing better than being able to sit out on a balcony or patio and be cooled by the night air. The atmosphere can be ruined, however, by a sudden attack of moths as they flicker around the only light source available, bouncing off your face and landing in your drink. A simple solution is to dissolve two tablespoons brown sugar in 250 ml/8 fl oz/1 cup hot water and add two tablespoons white vinegar. Place the mixture in a drinks can with the top cut off and put the can near the light but away from you. The moths will track down the scent of the sugar and stay away from the light and, more importantly, from you.

Other Garden Pests

Maintaining a garden offers great satisfaction but, if you are plagued by pests that keep devouring your fruits, vegetables and flowers, all your hard work will appear to have been in vain. The answer is to make a solution of 250 ml/8 fl oz/1 cup sugar, 250 ml/8 fl oz/1 cup vinegar, to which you add a banana skin, cut into pieces. Pour the mixture into an open plastic container and hang or place it near your prize plants. The fumes will attract the bugs, who will treat themselves to the contents of the container before promptly dying. Change the container and the mixture (and clear the dead bugs out) when necessary.

Seeds

Certain seeds can benefit from a little vinegar as they start to germinate. They include asparagus, okra, sweet peas, nasturtium, parsley and parsnip. Check with your local garden centre or hardware store for more types. Soaking the seeds overnight in warm water, vinegar and a shot of detergent will speed the sprouting process.

Flowers

It is wonderful to receive a bouquet but sad to have the flowers fall to a drooping mess two days later. The trick to keeping flowers for a longer period of time is to add two tablespoons vinegar and one teaspoon sugar to the water in the vase. If your flowers are starting to wilt, this mixture will bring them back to life.

After a period of time, vases acquire a water mark which doesn't seem to disappear no matter how many times you wash the vase. Soak a paper towel in white vinegar and place it in the vase, so that it covers the watermark. Leave for 30 minutes then wipe clean.

Acidic Plants

Certain plants love an acidic soil – strange but true. Plants such as azaleas, rhododendrons, hydrangeas and gardenias all thrive in an acidic soil. To keep these plants happy, add 250 ml/8 fl oz/1 cup white vinegar to 2 litres/3 1/2 pints/8 cups water and give them a drink every two to three weeks. Note that vinegar water is not beneficial to other plants. If you want to introduce any of the above acid plants into your garden, try watering the area with the same vinegar mixture for two to three weeks prior to planting them. This will create an acidic area for the plants so that, when you bring them into the garden, they will feel welcomed by the soil. Ensure that the area is isolated as a more acidic soil can harm other plants.

Vegetables

Growing your own vegetables is a wonderful and enriching process, especially eating the fruits of your labour. Once they are picked from the garden, wash them in a solution of one tablespoon white vinegar to 2 litres/3 1/2 pints/8 cups water. If there are any tiny insects from the garden, they will fall off the vegetables and the vinegar will disinfect and clean the produce.

Tools

Garden tools, however robust, will eventually rust through being used outdoors and may fall to pieces. They are easily cleaned by soaking overnight in standard household white vinegar with a 5% acetic acid content. The vinegar will stop the rusting and soon your tools will be shiny again.

You can also use gardening vinegar, but be careful how long you place the tool in the liquid as this acetic acid will burn much faster. You must also ensure that your skin is fully protected. Whichever vinegar you use, the tools need to be rinsed thoroughly in hot water and dried, or the vinegar will continue its action.

Garden Furniture

Outdoor furniture is always exposed to mildew and dirt. A clean-up is required to get your furniture ready for the summer season. For wood furniture, mix together 50 ml/2 fl oz/1/4 cup white vinegar, 1 tablespoon of baking soda and 1/2 cup ammonia in 2 litres/3 1/2 pints/8 cups water. Sponge the mixture on the furniture, leave for a minute and then scrub the stains away. Ensure you give it a final rinse in warm water to protect the wood.

Once dry, a final coating of oil or beeswax will ensure the longevity of the wood. For plastic or metal furniture, use one tablespoon of dish-washing liquid to 500 ml/16 fl oz/2 cups white vinegar in 2 litres/ 3 1/2 pints/8 cups hot water. Paint or sponge the mixture on to the furniture then scrub away the grime. Give the furniture a final rinse in hot water and leave to dry in the sun.

Gardener's Hands

Garden lime is used to enrich the soil but it is not very good for humans and can cause skin irritation and dryness. Rinse your hands thoroughly in white vinegar after use. If you grow berries in your back yard, when it is time to pick them the berry juices can stain your hands. Rub white vinegar into the stains and they will disappear. At the end of your working day in the garden, wash your hands in white vinegar. This will clean and disinfect them and get rid of any bacteria you may have picked up during the day.